Dream #2

We are riding in the back of a pickup truck. We are in Frankville, Alabama, where I lived until I was 12 years old. I always thought I would feel at home on New York City streets as I learned how to navigate them but I didn't — it is these dirt paths that I still know like they were etched on the inside of my skin, on the inside of my eyelids. How could anywhere but here ever be home? You are home with me. We are sitting on the wheel wells across from each other, the same way I used to do when I was a girl, I am older now but the pasture roads haven't changed. I feel where they are still muddy, sandy, gravelly as the tires send signals to my vibrating bones. Your great-grandfather, my Dandy, is driving, indigo along the way he does when he's checking on cows and things. He holds a Salem menthol out the rolled-down window and smoke wafts into my nose. He has known you your entire life and thinks you're a fine boy. He's especially proud when you wear the denim overalls you're wearing today. He died six years before you were born. We are in time and out of time. The sunshine hits your hair and it looks like gold. You squint your eyes as you look up to the sky. You are ageless. You are five years old. We drive away from Dry Creek and back toward Dandy's barn, passing the big old oak tree in the middle of the pasture. You say to me, "Look at that tree, Mama. It has so much moss hanging from it! I like it. I like it here." You are home with me. You are home to me.

Praise for Allison Moorer's *Blood*

"Beautiful, heart-wrenching . . . Moorer's masterful, comforting storytelling may serve as solace for those who've faced abuse, a signal for those in it to get out, and an eye-opener for others."

—*Publishers Weekly*, **starred review**

"Moorer's memoir is full of backstory-memories, current notes and thoughts, and well-described metaphors that come together fluidly, all told with grit and lyrical prose. . . . Her writing is beautiful and gripping and will stop readers in their tracks . . . a must-read."

—*Booklist*, **starred review**

"There is much wisdom in her experience as well as in her reflections on what she has read and heard. . . . Much different from most musicians' memoirs and of much interest to all who wrestle to understand tragedies of their own."

—*Kirkus Reviews*, **starred review**

"Allison Moorer is known for songs of ragged, poetic honesty—and for the emotional clarity of her country western ballads. Her debut memoir exhibits these qualities and more."

—*Literary Hub*,
One of the Most Anticipated Books of 2019

"There are few writers—few people, in fact—who could examine with such profound bravery the immense suffering and trauma in her story, infuse it with a lyrical sense of timelessness, and make us feel grateful for the telling. *Blood* is both unflinching and redemptive: a song of loss and courage."

—Rosanne Cash

"Like her songwriting, Moorer's prose is steeped in a rich sense of place, vivid characterization, and a story you will never forget. Not since Joan Didion's *Blue Nights* has grief been explored with so much beauty and complexity."

—Silas House, author of *Southernmost*

"Grit and grace, beauty and pain, on every wise page. Allison Moorer has given us a memoir as bloody, rich, and complex as red Alabama clay."

—Alice Randall, author of *The Wind Done Gone*

"*Blood* reveals the complicated mess of love and hurt that all too many readers will recognize. Moorer herself survived the unimaginable, and her poetic testimony should summon vigorous new attention to the public-health crisis that is male anger."

—Sarah Smarsh, author of *Heartland*

"*Blood* is the most vulnerable work you're likely to read for quite some time."

—Rick Bass, author of *For a Little While*

"[A] harrowing debut."

—*Elle*

"Her voice rings with equal parts defiance and vulnerability."

—*Blender*

"[Moorer's] written this book like a symphony. It is expansive, and its three parts feel like movements. Moorer fills them with prose that has the sharp honesty of the greatest songwriters."

—*The Bitter Southerner*

"Written with brave, clear-eyed compassion for all involved, *Blood* is an astonishing and moving meditation on family inheritance and acceptance. Despite her family's singularly tragic circumstances, *Blood* tells a universal story about the things our parents pass down to us—what we learn to be grateful for, what we release ourselves from, and what we simply leave alone."

—**Jennifer Palmieri,**
author of *Dear Madame President*

I
Dream
He
Talks
to Me

Also by Allison Moorer
Blood

I
Dream
He
Talks
to Me

A MEMOIR OF LEARNING
HOW TO LISTEN

Allison Moorer

New York

Hachette Books
Hachette Book Group
1290 Avenue of the Americas
New York, NY 10104
HachetteBooks.com
Twitter.com/HachetteBooks
Instagram.com/HachetteBooks

First Edition: October 2021

Published by Hachette Books, an imprint of Perseus Books, LLC, a subsidiary of Hachette Book Group, Inc. The Hachette Books name and logo is a trademark of the Hachette Book Group.

The Hachette Speakers Bureau provides a wide range of authors for speaking events. To find out more, go to www.hachettespeakersbureau.com or call (866) 376-6591.

The publisher is not responsible for websites (or their content) that are not owned by the publisher.

Print book interior design by Amy Quinn.

Library of Congress Cataloging-in-Publication Data
Names: Moorer, Allison, author.
Title: I dream he talks to me : a memoir of learning how to listen /
    Allison Moorer.
Description: First edition. | New York : Hachette Books, 2021.
Identifiers: LCCN 2021012467 | ISBN 9780306923074 (hardcover) | ISBN
    9780306923067 (ebook)
Subjects: LCSH: Moorer, Allison. | Singers—United States—Biography. |
    Mothers of autistic children—United States—Biography. | Autistic
    children—Family relationships—United States. | LCGFT: Autobiographies.
Classification: LCC ML420.M575 A3 2021 | DDC 782.42164092 [B]—dc23
LC record available at https://lccn.loc.gov/2021012467
ISBNs: 9780306923074 (hardcover), 9780306923067 (ebook)

Printed in the United States of America

LSC-C

Printing 1, 2021

Contents

Contents

For Mama.

Hope is not optimism, which expects things to turn out well, but something rooted in the conviction that there is good worth working for.

—Seamus Heaney

Dear John Henry,

I wasn't sure how you would feel about me telling people these things about us, so I wrote every word here imagining you were reading each one over my shoulder. There were days when writing them felt like the last thing I wanted to do, but I make art from my life. I don't always get to choose the content.

Some say an artist should never include her children in her work no matter the circumstances, that the best stories are the best just as much or more because of what you leave out of them rather than what you put in. But you are my work, my beloved son. You are my mind's resting place. You are my life. Sometimes the stories we love the most are our favorites because of what we're brave enough to leave in.

I can't remember who it was that once said to me, "You're one of those people with one of those lives," but I do remember not being able to argue that urgent and important things have happened. They still do. Those happenings inevitably require a response from me, and the best one I can offer is to try to turn them and their effects into something I can present back and whisper, "Here's what I've faced. Here's what I've learned from it. You are not alone in how you feel. No matter what it is, it can be okay." That's the most honorable way I've figured out how to be of help or service in this world. More than any other person or event, you have taught me, and you have changed me just by being you. You have been doing that since the day you were born. You will continue to do that until the day I die. So I can't imagine keeping to myself what a profound effect you've had on who I am. That is the most urgent and important of all the things that have happened. I figure you're okay with people knowing that and understand that if I left you out of the stories I tell, I'd be leaving them mostly untold because you are, in fact, the constant coauthor of my life now.

My gratitude to you feels endless, but I want to thank you most of all for showing me that the best way to love a person is to let them be exactly who they are. And just so you know, exactly who you are is perfect. I hope you don't mind if that's something I shout from the rooftops.

I love you.
Mama
Nashville, Tennessee
November 2020

Below the Belt

There's a place in the human singing voice right around the top of the middle that can sound like a bell. It's a mixture of chest and head voice. I've always called it the "mid-belt"—where you can get a significant amount of air, or power, behind a note and belt it out, as they say. It vibrates in the body that makes it, and in the air that it hits.

John Henry's father and I are both singer-songwriters, and we were on an extended tour together the summer John Henry started walking. One particular August Sunday we didn't have a show to do, so I played with John Henry in the tour bus and half-heartedly watched *60 Minutes*. When the show aired a profile of a teenage gospel choir, my interest grew. The choir was singing "Amazing Grace." I sang along, but when I got to the "a" before the word "wretch" in the first verse, John Henry pushed his tiny hands into my chest and his face away from mine. I had held the mid-belt note for a little bit too long. His face broke, and he cried. I stopped singing. He was sixteen months old.

～

Music makes me cry too. I am often overwhelmed by the beauty or emotional resonance of a voice or composition. I've considered it one of my more annoying afflictions— that I can become a sobbing mess when I hear a certain vocal tone or a particularly beautiful conglomeration of notes.

But I had never seen that response in a toddler. And what I saw in John Henry that Sunday afternoon wasn't a feature of his personality. It wasn't a development. It was more as if something had gone missing.

I had seen him display little behaviors that I thought were maybe odd. He had a tendency to repeatedly turn objects over in his hands or play with one part of a toy instead of its entirety. He would rub his legs together against textured floor surfaces or in the bathtub as soon as he could sit on his own—we called it "crickets." But I didn't know that Sunday afternoon that I was looking at a human being who couldn't manage the information he received in a typical fashion. I didn't know it until I saw him burst into what I could tell were tears of emotion when I hit that note. I didn't know it until my mind raced around wondering why he'd cried them, and then realized that he had been using his words less and less in the weeks that preceded that day, that he had shuddered when he heard the drum kit on the Friday before at sound check, and that he had stopped turning his head toward anyone who said his name. I didn't know until then that my baby very likely had autism. Music has provided myriad revelations for me throughout my life, but this was one I didn't welcome.

꙳

I tried everything I could think of to bring him back. Several times each day, I practiced with him the words he had learned, even more than I had before. I tried to teach him new ones and would tentatively allow a wave of relief to come over me when he would try to imitate sounds and said things such as "key" for *turkey*, or "bala" for *banana*. I dutifully logged his behaviors, any little thing he uttered that sounded like a word, and any acknowledgment of another person. I tried to convince myself that what was happening wasn't happening, all the while confirming that it was indeed happening when I would check the lists of features of autism that I found on the internet against his progressing distance from who he had been.

I began calling doctors. Then we started down the road to an official diagnosis despite everyone, his pediatrician included, telling me that my sweet and social child couldn't possibly have autism. "Just look at him. There's no way he could be autistic," she said. John Henry began speech and occupational therapy, and even his speech therapist suggested that he had a sensory processing disorder and not autism, though his words had almost completely gone away by the time we made our way to her.

❧

He received the diagnosis the following March when he was administered the usual battery of tests that determine whether a person lands on the spectrum or not. By that time, we'd started to adjust to the reality that we'd likely be told he did. I had stopped singing in my full voice around John Henry. I would sing the baby songs—"B-I-N-G-O," "Twinkle, Twinkle, Little Star," and others that don't require any velocity—and he didn't seem to mind. But if a song or my voice held any hint of poignancy or hit that mid-belt place, it was too much for him. I was careful not to forget myself and break into song, as I had been wont to do for as long as I could remember. It was heart-breaking. I knew it wasn't about volume or pitch. It was about his becoming overwhelmed by the way my singing made him feel. If a human face is the hardest thing in the world to look at because it is so complicated and holds so much information, then the human voice must be the hardest thing to hear and make sense of for the same reasons. It all made me turn quiet. I felt as if we had lost a way to bond on top of everything else.

I thought John Henry might shy away from music for his entire life. I couldn't imagine what that would be like for a person, let alone one who was born into the family that he was. I didn't know and couldn't imagine an existence without it. I struggled with his struggle and I worried about what his father and I had passed on to him. Could it have been our faults that he was so sensitive to music? Music above all else has always given us both pathways with which to connect to the world. It has, in different ways, saved us. What we cannot say, we can sing. I thought it ironic that the son of two people whom music had blessed so richly was so plowed over by it. But as I got used to the idea that my son was very likely going to walk through this life with a different filter than most, I also started to see that he had a gift. I began to see that he didn't have a lack of love for music at all. In fact, it was the opposite. John Henry has a great sensitivity—it's almost as if he is missing a layer of protection against the onslaught of information the world can throw at you—but he slowly strengthened himself and continues to do so. I will always remember the day that I forgot to skip "The Cow Song" on his *Classical Baby* DVD (Puccini's "O mio babbino caro") and I found him standing in front of the television, little fists clenched, not just enthralled but also seemingly determined not to cry. He made it through the song without shedding a tear for the first time. I can't say the same for myself when I discovered him watching it, having come around the corner just a little too late.

෴

Now as we learn sign language together, the sign for *music* is one that I can almost always count on him to remember. He has no functional verbal language yet, but he sings to himself in what sounds to me like awfully good pitch. He strums his ukulele and plays the drums. He has rhythm, and its patterns seem to organize and regulate him. He likes Justin Bieber, OK Go, Hoagy Carmichael, Ravi Shankar, Adele (he simply beams when he hears her, which delights me), and Mozart. And to my great relief, he tolerates and shows signs of liking even his mama's singing.

What he once couldn't process at all now gets him through rough spots. If he becomes frustrated or upset, I turn to music to soothe him. If I want him to pay attention to me, I sing to him. We play records in the house and practice silly dances. What I know now that I didn't know on that August 2011 afternoon is that because his antenna is set so high, he can feel music deeply. It moves him. I often wonder what it is that he hears as he turns his head toward a tree when the wind rustles its leaves, or when he notices a formation of birds flying overhead and he smiles. I suspect he hears music all around him because he stops what he's doing and he listens. My son has taught me countless lessons, but the biggest one may be that there is music in everything. I don't know what role it will ultimately play in his life, whether he will pursue it professionally or if he will just enjoy it. I only know that music might very well be his language in some way. What he cannot say, he might one day sing too.

The Feeling Foot

The left shoe is always the first to come off. Sometimes it's the left one only. He has the routine perfected now—when he stands still, he starts to shimmy it off. Right toes on the heel of left shoe, press right toes down, lift heel of left foot, and voilà! Off it comes. He then proceeds to joyously prance and run around, his left foot seemingly taking the lead, piloting his often mysterious mission.

My son has, since he was born, appeared to prefer his feet bare, but during the past few years it's been hard to keep shoes on him at all. His teachers prescribed Chuck Taylor All Star high-tops, and they do work to alleviate the problem of constant removal as he is unable to thwart the double-tied laces, but it is now summertime. It is hot. I know that I wouldn't want my feet encased in thick terry cloth and canvas all day every day so I buy him sandals. I can tell it frustrates the teachers because he gets them off swiftly and they have to repeatedly help him put them back on his feet. All I can say about that is he wants his feeling foot free and I'm inclined to side with him.

I call it his "feeling foot" because that seems to be how he uses it—as one would their right index finger, as Sacajawea to the Lewis and Clark that is the rest of him. I watch and try to imagine why it goes ahead, how it steers him, and what it divines. Does it have a sensitivity that his other foot doesn't? Does the shoe hurt it? Is there a simple answer? Maybe.

He isn't a toe walker like some people with autism and sensory processing difficulties. Occupational therapists say that those with autism can't necessarily feel where their bodies are in space, that they have no specific sense of what their physical selves are always doing, that the vestibular system doesn't work properly. There lies the root of the personal space issues, the coordination problems, the lack of awareness, and the lack, or presence, of fear. Or not. It crosses my mind that my son doesn't have those problems in abundance, if at all. I wonder if he sits exactly where he wants, if he moves precisely as his instincts tell him, and if he is perfectly aware that there's nothing at all, in a cosmic sense, to be afraid of.

What am I afraid of? Why do I watch him so closely? I'm afraid I will miss something, and it's my job to know everything. I watch him closely so that I might see.

I try to see. I stand back and I observe. As I do, I'm acutely aware that I am not interacting, rather studying him as if I need to take notes for a test. Indeed, this is a test of sorts, of my intelligence, my deductive reasoning power, my empathy, my sympathy, my humanity, my capacity for love. I desperately want to not just pass but earn an A. An A-plus. I want to wrangle my skills and master my subject, earn an advanced degree, become an expert in it, confidently converse about its many misunderstood nooks and under-thought-about crannies. The feeling foot is my syllabus.

The shoe comes off. The prancing, the excitement, the jumping, the running, the flapping of the hands and the bare foot onto the wood floor, the grass, or the concrete. Does the texture register through his nerves and skin? Does the wood feel smooth and warm, the grass prickly, and the concrete scratchy and hot? I think about my own left foot. My feet are outrageously ticklish and sensitive on the bottoms, yet toughened on the balls and heels from years of cruel shoes and Manhattan living—I walk, therefore I am. I walk in heels, therefore I haven't yet given up. I rub my bare foot over the rug on the floor below where I sit. Soft, fluffy, a little warmer than the rest of the room. Would his foot feel what mine does? If it didn't, what is our framework for commonality? Where do our ideas meet if we don't discover we have similar experiences? How do I know him if he is unlike me? I look for common ground. He rids himself of the left shoe and twirls in the gym of his school, sits on the front porch of the house in Nashville, or splashes in a puddle. *More time with no shoes on*, I think.

To know is to be familiar, to have the information, the data, the raw material with which to take the next action. Parents, when we have new babies, spend most of our time trying to gather evidence about them so we'll understand what to do and then what to do next. We want to be familiar, to understand. To be understood is to be comforted. We deduct, we reason, we work the problem, we solve the puzzle so that we can console or help, so we can be the ones *who know*. We wait for the talking to start and think it will tell us more. But what if the luxury of language doesn't appear? Can we still know? Can I know my son if he doesn't use words?

He doesn't have to say it. He has conveyed his love of barefootedness to me without so much as an *a*, *b*, or *c*. I think of words—their magic, their ordinariness, their successfulness, and their utter failure. If he could talk, maybe he would say, "I much prefer to have my left foot unshod than trapped in this stifling sneaker. I want to feel the earth, the floor, and where I'm going." But he doesn't have to. He is more efficient than that and has figured out how to get what he wants without having to make a verbal, or any kind of, request. Would he tell me what that foot feels even if he could? Words fail. Actions communicate clearly.

༄

I grab his foot and tickle it. He jerks it back. He playfully sticks it back out and toward my hand. I grab it and tickle it again. He laughs. Communication. We are playing. His foot is ticklish like mine. His foot is like mine. He is like me. We are related. I know his foot. Common ground. I know him.

The feeling foot flaps on the concrete front porch. Joy, exploration, serenity, smooth cool stone, or maybe, "I don't want to go anywhere. I want to stay right here on this porch where it is cool and there's a breeze and I can smell the grass and flowers and hear the birds." He climbs into the swing. I sit down beside him. I am quiet and so is he. I listen. Like the feeling foot, I am suddenly bare, unguarded, and open, seeking the information that will guide me toward the answer to the next thing. Like the feeling foot, I go ahead, looking for what's in front of us.

A Guide to Getting Through

1. Keep your perspective.

It will be helpful to you if you have already lived through some life-altering events that will have shown you how to do this autism thing more easily. Of course, having a child with autism will be nothing like any of the things you thought you wouldn't live through before you did, but it will be monumental in your life. It will shake you to your core and you will have to figure it out daily. But look at the bright side—if you have been lucky enough to have had even one reality-shattering event upend your life before now, you will have developed a few fuck-it skills. Because of them, you will know not to ask, "Why me?" You will instead, when you figure a few things out, say, "Well, why *not* me? I got this."

2. Get used to not sleeping.

There will be nights when your child won't go to bed and stay there. There will be nights when you will wake up and he's standing over you, staring. There will be nights when you will wake up and sense something is amiss, go to his room, and find him standing in the windowsill looking down to the courtyard four stories below. There will be nights when you'll wake to the sound of water running. There will be nights when you will have the what-ifs so bad that it will be you who won't be able to keep your eyes closed. Then there will be nights when he just wants to crawl in bed and cuddle with you. Those will keep you awake too, either because you'll be happily staring at him or because you'll be clinging to the edge of the mattress since you don't want to wake him and he's taking up the entire bed.

3. Grow elephant-sized balls.

And flip the bird, either literally or just in your imagination, to everyone who gives you shocked looks when your child disrobes in public. The same goes for when he joyously jumps into a large decorative fountain, swipes food off of a complete stranger's plate in a restaurant, darts around like a hyena in a movie theater maniacally laughing and throwing popcorn, jerks clothing off of a hanger at a store and whips it around like an adrenaline-crazed matador in front of a bull, screams at the top of his lungs while on an airplane for seemingly no reason (there's always a reason, by the way, you just won't always know what it is), or generally wreaks unimaginable havoc in a public place. Sometimes people need to get over it and see that you have your hands too full to stop and explain everything all the time.

4. Be okay with being lonely.

You might sometimes feel isolated from those in your life who don't quite understand your challenges, and even from those who do. Sometimes what's going on will be impossible to explain. Sometimes you'll just be too tired to try. You might start talking to yourself, thinking there's nothing weird about doing so. After all, it's strange to live with another person who doesn't ever answer your questions and hardly ever utters a word at all. You will still have friends, but you will often be too tired to accept their invitations, or they, like you (because birds of a feather), will have a child they can't leave for long either. Try to remember yourself and take a breather when you are allowed. Have a real conversation about something other than autism, or have a cup of coffee with someone who *does* get it and discuss it at length.

5. Don't shrink.

You're going to have to expand. You're going to have to stand up for your child to the fullest degree. There will be no "working it out on the playground" if another kid bullies yours. You will surprise yourself and want to throttle the little devil who dares to make fun of your baby's arm flapping or distinctive vocal sounds. This instinct applies to more organized situations and institutions as well. When the speech and language department tells you that your non-speaking child is going to have his fifth new speech therapist in less than four years, you're going to have to meet with the Head of School and say it's not acceptable. When you have to take "I know" for an answer, you will walk, fuming, out of the building and consider impaling yourself on the pointy end of one of the pickets of the wrought-iron fence surrounding the park that he can't play in even though it's next to his school. You're going to have to remember that thankfulness and a bottomless well of gratitude is not always the answer. You will have to demand what you know your child needs, even to the supposed experts.

6. Nod and smile.
"Is he talking yet?"
"So, is he really good at music?"
"I'll bet he's a math whiz."
"Oh, I can tell he's so smart."

7. Be okay with wasting money.
You will buy every book on autism. You will visit doctors whom friends have told you helped their child. You will try special diet after special diet thinking there might be something to the leaky gut theory. You will pay more at the grocery store than you ever thought possible save for when you shopped for Thanksgiving dinner in 2008 and you were feeding twelve people. You will go

to the health-food store and buy magnesium, B12, B6, L-glutamine, turmeric, etcetera, etcetera, and every soothing essential oil and natural remedy until your cabinets smell like an old hippie's. You will try anything that holds a promise. You won't care how much it costs. You will eventually learn that none of it really makes that much difference, not that much more or even as much as it would in a so-called neurotypical person, except for the essential oils and aromatherapy. At least they make you and your house smell nice.

8. Learn how to swim through snake oil.

You will nod and smile (see number 6) when some well-meaning person tells you about an article they read or a video they saw about how someone cured their child of autism. You will already know about it because you will have started to do a Google search on the latest news and developments in the land of ASD every morning while you sip your first cup of coffee. You will be curious about the reports that might hold some real promise, but you will know that those are, sadly, few and far between.

9. Practice selective deafness.

You might, from time to time, overhear someone whisper, "What is wrong with that child?" You might, early on, try to tell them that there's nothing wrong, he only has autism. Chances are you'll quickly develop a sort of shield for your ears and will begin to slightly block out the ugly utterances, murmurings, hisses, and sighs. If you don't, you will at least tell yourself that the remarks don't matter even as your heart breaks. You will tell yourself your child can't hear them too. You will probably be wrong.

10. Get help if you need it.

I didn't think I would need any at first. I thought I'd be able to power my way through this like everything else in my life (see number 1). But this isn't everything else. The panic attacks and sleeplessness started for me even before he was diagnosed. The feeling of dread about what was around the next corner that I carried already suddenly deepened with the realization that the unthinkable was not only thinkable but our actual reality. I'd wake up just to watch him breathe. Sometimes, I still do. The post-traumatic stress disorder I've tussled with my entire life kicked back in after he *was* diagnosed, full throttle. I had dreams about earthquakes, about being stuck underground, and that was when I slept deeply enough to dream at all. I got a therapist and try not to think about taking a nerve pill here and there being a possible cause of dementia because I will not be taking them for very much longer, as soon as he gets better, as soon as he starts to talk, as soon as I'm not working so hard, as soon as . . .

11. Lose all fear of embarrassment.

This will free you and make your life better in some ways, though you might miss your old sense of decorum. When your child melts down in the airport while sitting in your lap at the gate after you've asked for pre-boarding privileges so you can get settled before everyone else and alert the flight attendants about what the possibilities are for their next shift, then he reaches behind him and yanks your hair so hard you think there's no way you could have any left and accompanies this with some ear-piercing screams and the toss of his bottle of water six feet in front of him, just block out the world. Forget that there is anyone looking at you and stare at the floor or straight ahead while you comfort your child because he is most definitely uncomfortable and getting him soothed is your priority. Forget that they most likely don't understand what they're seeing. Forget that they might think you're a terrible mother with a spoiled, out-of-control child. Forget that they might not stop to think that he may be tired or off his schedule, that their perfume might be making his olfactory nerves feel like they've been plugged into an electrical socket, or that the flickering fluorescent lights might be giving him a migraine. Your child is going to embarrass you. You will need to remember that no child has ever failed to embarrass his parent. You're just going to get a little extra some days. Learn to deal with it with as much grace as possible. You will get through it and maybe even laugh about it later. And if anyone says anything to you about it, you will shut them down with something like this: "He has autism. We're doing the best we can."

12. Find peace in sometimes letting it go and letting it be.
You won't always want to correct or redirect. You will sometimes want to let him be who he is, even if who he is

flaps his hands, twirls until he falls over, takes seven baths a day, listens to the same song and watches the same movie repeatedly because it makes him happy to do so. There will be days you simply won't have the energy or will to do anything else. Besides, who among us does not have an odd habit or two that we can't help but practice? Are we not all peculiar in some way? Do we not all want to scream at the top of our lungs in airports? We could take a tip or two from the unfiltered.

13. Eat alphabet soup every meal of the day.

ASD, EI, CPSE, IEP, CSE, BOE, ABA, DIR, IDEA, FAPE, ADA, LRE, PECS, DRO, SLP, BCBA, OT, BIP, AAC, APE, ASL, GFCF, PDD, PDD-NOS, PP, PT . . . You will be surprised at how quickly you catch on to these acronyms and the amount of ease with which you will begin to use them.

14. Be proud of the little things.

Any small victory will make you happier than you can believe. Any success or mastery is cause for a party because you will know how hard your child struggled to achieve it. A word spoken might make you jump up and down and decide a breakthrough is impending. That's okay. You are entitled to be excited. Don't take that joy away from yourself by thinking you're not supposed to be happy because the word might slip back away, that it's too disappointing when something doesn't end up being the leap forward you thought it might be. You will learn to revel in the tiniest progress even if it does fade back out of sight. You will smile through your tears of joy and say, "Today, John Henry said 'apple' when he saw one." Don't let your hope fizzle. Be proud of him. He's probably having a harder time than you can even imagine.

15. Don't begrudge others their big things.

Try to step outside of your world now and then and listen to others tout their children's accomplishments. No one sails through this world problem-free. Celebrate when someone tells you her daughter got into Brown or is getting married. Everyone has a path. Have faith that the one you're on is leading your family where it needs to be, even if it feels dark and circular some days.

16. Protect more fiercely than you ever thought you could.

Do you remember the urge you had to physically shield your baby when he was an infant? It won't go away. There is an innocence that comes with autism that is dangerous. Our sensory-seeking children will run away from us, climb bookshelves, topple furniture, put everything in their mouths, lick subway poles, jump into any body of water, trust strangers, and generally keep us on alert and looking for the next ten potential hazards. You will feel panicky when he is out of your sight. Our sensory-avoiding children will put their hands over their ears upon hearing any loud noise, melt down over a tag in a shirt, and refuse to take medicine. You will go to surprising lengths to ensure those invaders do not reach your child's nerves. You won't be able to bat back all of them. Most every parent has the instinct to defend. Yours will be elevated to a level that may surprise you. Refer back to number 5. You will stand between him and the world.

17. Embrace being mad sometimes.

Sometimes anger will be all that will get you through the day. And the next one. It will occasionally be difficult not to embody your emotions but that's okay—your rage will probably eventually ease. My experience is that the intensity of it all ebbs and flows. Try to take ample care of yourself when you have the chance. That will be a challenge, but it's one that is necessary for you to take on not only for your health but for everyone's.

18. Laugh.

There will be times when you have no choice: when you have poop or something worse all over your hands or even your face, when the iPad goes sailing through the air at a special sensory-friendly performance of *The Lion King* or off the balcony of a hotel room, when the brand-new sneakers are soaked with mud because a puddle was simply irresistible, when the neighbor complains about the noise coming from the floor above their head for the thirteenth time. Try to find some shred of humor in the absurdity of the idea that everything in life, not just yours, isn't utter chaos. Remember every moment, no matter how harrowing, is fleeting. It will change. This is a marathon, not a sprint.

When You Stare

From an evolutionary perspective, staring indicates dominance. Someone wants to assert power, so they lock their eyes on the threat. The object interprets that they are somehow inferior and cowers.

Whether my son feels that way or not, I don't know. He doesn't seem to. But I do realize his face might not register the expected expression to go along with his emotions. That you would potentially hurt him, that you would try to make him feel inferior, even subconsciously, boils my blood. I'm sure that when you stare you don't think that's what you're doing. Yes, I'm quite sure you're not thinking about that.

Whether you know that's what you're doing or not, maybe your undivided attention just bolsters the sense of cool that he already has. I hope he thinks something like this: *Look at that jackass staring at me. They're so inhibited they don't know how to take in the awesome being that I am since I'm being my full-on self and theirs got tamped down in them for some reason.* I pray for that. I also doubt that. I sometimes think I see his face fall just a little bit when he feels someone boring holes into him with their eyes. He gets a little quieter, his movements become a little bit smaller. Some would argue that that's a good thing, but I would suggest someone changing himself due to another's disapproval only serves to make us all go more toward the middle. I don't think that's the direction in which we're supposed to be heading.

∽

Most days I think I'd like for my son to have a more typical experience. Some features of autism are decidedly not desirable. But who am I to say? What if he's having the time of his life? What if the things that bother the rest of us don't bother him so much? What if he's experiencing a fantasia phantasmagoria in his mind and we just disturb it with our demands on him to become more like we are? I remember saying to someone, when he was newly diagnosed, that I'd love for him to be able to sit and turn a block between his hands all day every day because that seemed to be what made him feel good, but that unfortunately this was not a world of block turners and I was going to have to do my best to get him off of block-turner island. Though we've made some strides there, at the time I said it I thought we'd have made more by now. John Henry is a block turner. Just as we all have our things, he will always have his.

Yes, you certainly have your things. Maybe your in-
cessant throat clearing strikes me as odd, your constant
nose wiping, repulsive. Maybe your verbal tics and slue-
footedness make me want to cross to the other side of the
street. But I wouldn't want to make you feel self-conscious
or uncomfortable.

I want to stare back at you when you stare at him. I
want to imitate your face with my face and show you how
ridiculous and awful you look—eyes bulging, jaw slack
with incredulity. But I don't, not usually, not unless I'm
in a particularly perturbed mood and think I desire some
sort of confrontation, which I know you would refuse. If
I said or did something to acknowledge your lack of gra-
ciousness, you'd probably act surprised and scurry away
from us, thinking I was in the wrong. But I don't usually
stare back unless I've got a lot of starch in my britches that
day. Not only because I want to keep my son focused on
being his most liberated self and how I don't think he's
strange—of course I want to do that—but also because I
know it's not polite. Clearly, someone forgot to tell you
that. Or maybe you were told and you just forgot.

I've never known more than I know now that most
people are completely thrown by things that are out of
their ordinary. Just as I am sometimes surprised by children who speak, most folks are surprised by the fact that
mine does not—yet—communicate clearly with words.
Or that he still needs to be reminded to go to the bathroom sometimes, that he occasionally prefers to eat with
his hands instead of the proper utensil if it's more efficient

for him, that he doesn't play video games on his iPad and instead watches movies and listens to music, and that he doesn't care to play soccer and instead wants to swim all day every day because his body feels free and right in the water.

You appear intrigued by his differences. I do wonder, though, why you need to stare. Are you horrified by autism? Do you know that's what you're seeing, and not a spoiled child who runs roughshod over his mother? He may very well be spoiled. I'd admittedly try to lasso the moon for him if I thought it would make him happy, but that's not what's happening here. What you're seeing is a boy living inside his own world, and a mama who can't find the key to let herself in or him out or even the instructions that might help him do either himself. Imagine how it feels for us to be struggling to get through a moment and then add the insult of thinking you're probably thinking we're doing a bad job and we're disturbing you.

I try to put away my concern over what others think and just keep it where it needs to be, on him. But as hard as I try to be, I am not superhuman. I can think of very few people on the planet who are not at least given pause by hurtful remarks or looks of disdain. And I can think of no one who can escape a raised heart rate when those things are directed at her child.

Maybe you're just curious. Maybe you aren't like the man at the pool who shouts at us when John Henry is loud or the woman who asks if he "has to make that noise?" Maybe you want to ask a question but you're afraid of offending me. Maybe you want to offer help but don't know what kind to offer. You know what you could do that might help? Be kind. Please try to understand something that is, yes, un-understandable to you. And please know this—we are not inferior, but we fight feeling that way. Sometimes it's a major effort to get through not just the day, but even the hour, even the minute. My son is, I pray, safe in the knowledge that he is protected and secure, but the lengths to which I go to make sure of those things feel extreme some days. We don't need added pressure from you. If you want to ask me something, please do. I will answer you as kindly as possible if I can.

We're doing the best we can. If you want to look, try to smile at us. Smile at us and the effort we're making to get along. And if you feel like it, tell us we're beautiful and that we're doing just fine.

Fine

Alex, the daytime doorman at our building, has known us almost two years now, since we moved in when John Henry was four. He's never said anything outside of "Good morning" or "How are you?" to us before. But today, after I returned from the walk to school, he stopped me before I got in the elevator.

He struggled to find the words he wanted to use. He held his hands apart, and his forefingers touched his thumbs as if he were about to conduct an orchestra in playing a soothing, low om tone. He hesitated, then said, "I see you with your son. He will be fine by the time he is twelve, thirteen. I've seen boys like him in my home country. They always get better by then."

"Twelve or thirteen?"

"Yes. He will be okay by then."

I smiled at him, nodded, stepped into the elevator, and hit the button for the fourth floor. I held in my hand the mail I'd stopped to get from the box, and held the tears inside my eyes to keep them from falling down my face. My night and morning had been a little rough.

∽

Every doorknob in our apartment has chimes or bells hanging from it. Should John Henry decide to get up and move around past his bedroom door during the night, their sound lets me know. This morning, I woke at 1:30 to the clanging of the chimes hanging from the door that separates our bedrooms from the rest of our apartment. When I heard them, I left my warm bed and anxiously took the nine or ten steps it takes to get from my bedroom to his. I stood at the doorway and peered through foggy eyes at him jumping around his room. I stepped in, took his hand, and led him through the hallway door to the bathroom. We took care of business, then returned to his bedroom, and I told him to go back to bed. I relocked the hallway door behind us as I always do to prevent him from going into the rest of the apartment lest he raid the refrigerator or something else (I call this "raccooning"), then I lay down beside him on his bottom bunk, with him on the inside, next to the wall. Sometimes if I lie down with him, it helps him go back to sleep.

I woke an hour or so later to him gone and the sound of objects being thrown. He was on his top bunk, happily chucking a few toys that were stored up there to the floor.

I coaxed him down and told him he needed to go back to bed. He complied and snuggled into the bottom bunk. I snuggled in with him.

My eyes fluttered open again at 4:30 a.m. He wasn't beside me. He wasn't anywhere in the room. I suspected I'd made him feel crowded and he'd gone down the hall to take over my spot in my bed, so I got up again, walked down the hallway, and found him snuggled but awake among some pillows on my bedroom floor, laughing. I pulled him by the hand to an upright position and took him back to his room one more time. I didn't say anything. I guess I gave up talking in my exhausted state. I got him re-tucked into his bed, then myself finally tucked back into my own for what I hoped would be an hour of sleep before my alarm went off to tell me to rise, get the coffee made and breakfast started, the lunch box filled, the inbox checked, and that night's graduate seminar final projects looked over and completed.

A few naps nestled themselves into fifty-five minutes and I finally rose for good at 5:25. I stopped by my son's bedroom on the way to the kitchen and was pleased to find him sleeping. *Good*, I thought, *I can have a little time alone, and I know he needs to rest to have a decent day at school.* I resented him only a little, and even that faded by the time I got to the living room, which took five seconds at most. I can't stay mad or even put out for very long, no matter how he tests me or how little sleep I get.

❧

I like to wake the house up slowly and ease into the day with as much softness as I'm able, especially if the night has been less than peaceful. My soothing rituals afford me a counterbalance to the madness I sometimes experience. Parenting is a tough job. Parenting a child with special needs is an especially tough job sometimes and I find little sanities everywhere I can. I get the kettle on to boil for my daily large French press of coffee first thing, then set about turning on lamps and fluffing the living room to make it warm and inviting. The two floor lamps on either side of the big sofa go on first, then the small lamp on top of the bookcase by the dining table, then the one on top of the bookcase by my desk. The living room glows and comforts me in this calm hour. It's overfilled and cluttered with books, art, artifacts, and other signs of our busy life, but it's home, and I'm thankful for it. This morning, I silently counted my blessings as I cut up an apple for my boy. He'd have half for breakfast, and I put the other half in the lunch box that would accompany him to school.

He's on a new diet these days, one recommended by a highly respected developmental pediatrician we've seen a few times. No wheat, no sugar, and no fruit or vegetables high in acidity. Apples are okay. Oranges are not. The doctor thinks the diet, along with two kinds of probiotics that help rid the stomach of yeast, might help heal my son's gut and ease his almost constant digestive issues. So far, no luck. I've seen a slight change here and there, but nothing significant. I wondered why again this morning when, after I had finally gotten him dressed and he was already an hour late for school because I let him sleep due to his being awake for so long during the night, I had to change his outfit because of another episode that occurred just before I took him to the bathroom—always our last stop before we head out for our short walk to school. My heart broke over what is certainly at least an uncomfortable problem for my child and what is quite possibly a bigger embarrassment than I can fathom, but we got on with things, as we do, and made it to school with no incidents. After we did, I turned him over to his head teacher, then made my way back to our building.

ꙮ

He will be fine by the time he is twelve, thirteen.

ꙮ

He is six years old now, almost seven. What will life be like five or six years from now? What will he be like? What will I be like? Where will we be? How will we live?

What if he isn't fine?

What *is* fine?

Would fine mean he speaks in a language everyone else can understand? How many words would his sentences have to have? Would fine mean that he never gets up in the night? Some people aren't good sleepers and they're considered fine. Would fine mean that he is like every other person? Because no person is like any other person. I am like no one else, yet I am considered fine. And I know plenty of people who appear to be fine but who are definitely not fine. Where is the line between fine and not fine and who decides where it lies?

There are so many things that I want for my son—the ability to express himself, care for himself, one day live independently, have a job or fulfilling work, a life partner or partners or someone who is his person or some some-ones who are his people forever and ever amen. Does he have to be fine to have those things, and would his having those things in turn make him what is considered fine? Is having those things what makes most of us seem fine? Is seeming fine what enables most of us to have those things? One has to be fine to get those things. One has to have those things to be considered fine. I try to follow the thought all the way to the end but it doesn't work. It turns circular and in on itself, collapsing like all the parameters around the concept of fine do when you poke at them.

My son's autism doesn't have to lead to a life of less than others have. Where is it written that he has to have fewer opportunities, less fulfillment, or scarcer and more insuf-ficient happiness than those considered fine are entitled to because he has a disability? He may not be what the world at large would consider fine by the time he is twelve or thirteen, or twenty or thirty, but if I have anything to do with it, he will not have or be less.

In any case, of course I yearn for Alex to be right. Isn't it remarkable that one person saying one thing can skew our vision toward that thing? I think of the boys to whom he was referring and them having gotten better. I know John Henry can get better too. I then remember we've got a long way to go, because now? Now he might put his head in the toilet if I'm in the kitchen cooking us something to eat. Facedown. In the toilet. What am I supposed to do about that when I need to leave the lid up so he can use it properly and independently more easily? The behavior will pass. They always do and another one will replace it.

Alex doesn't know about the head in the toilet. Alex doesn't know about a lot of things. He doesn't know about the Level 3 diagnosis, does he? Level 3 is the most severe. Were the boys he was referring to having gotten better by the time they were twelve or thirteen diagnosed as Level 3?

Autistic people with Level 3 autism need the most support compared to Levels 1 and 2. They might find it very difficult to use or understand verbal and nonverbal communication.

The person may:

- avoid or limit interaction with others
- find it difficult to play or engage with others
- show limited interests
- engage in self-stimulatory behavior (stimming) or have repetitive behaviors, such as flicking the fingers (non-contextual hand movements), to the point that it affects their ability to pay attention to anything else
- experience a high level of distress if their routine or environment is changed

Autism can have both social and behavioral effects on an individual.

In social situations, they may find the following difficult:

- following directions
- making and maintaining eye contact
- controlling impulses
- using facial expressions that match the context of communication
- understanding another person's feelings
- understanding that certain situations pose dangers, i.e., heights, water

The person's behavior may include:

- self-stimulatory behaviors and compulsivity, such as rocking from side to side or doing the same thing over and over again
- developing a high level of skill in certain areas—i.e., some sort of savantism
- paying attention to only specific parts of an object, such as the wheels on a toy car
- being more or less sensitive to sensory stimulation—such as loud noises—compared with neurotypical people
- having sleep problems

In some cases, autism may affect a person's balance, coordination, motor skills, and muscle tone.

I know what Alex sees, and it isn't Level 3. He sees a beautiful, sweet boy who stops to observe him and sometimes smiles when we pass by his desk in the mornings, not someone who doesn't make eye contact. He hears about the hugs that Apu, the second-shift doorman, receives when we come in from school in the afternoons and he invites us to look at the security-camera screens behind the counter, not someone who has difficulty forming friendships. He sees an open face, one that tilts toward the sky when we walk through the door of the building and onto the steps that lead us to the sidewalk that will take us wherever we're going, not someone who has limited interests. He sees my son run and jump and be happy in the hallways, not someone who has difficulty with balance, coordination, and motor skills. He sees him hold my hand and trust that I'm leading him somewhere worthwhile, not someone who has difficulty coping with changes to his routine or environment.

Alex sees John Henry. Alex sees hope. Alex sees someone who will be fine, and so do I. Even on a morning when I am under-rested, worried, and feel like crawling under the bed and sleeping for a good long while.

⚬⚬⚬

I wonder if those boys Alex knew in his home country had any kind of diagnoses? That's one of the problems with diagnoses, and with the resulting categories into which we file people away. Once we organize the collected data into an understandable system, we think we've solved at least that part of this confounding problem. But people aren't reducible to a category because the tests don't ask for all the details. The tests don't account for the fact that for every Level 3 trait my son has, there are just as many contradictions to the idea that he will always need constant support.

- The rare—but even if a thing is rare it still exists—pop-out words.
- The independent bathroom trips and burgeoning executive functioning skills.
- The melodies he makes up, remembers, and sings back and forth with me in a conversational manner.
- The swiftness with which he can display his highest skills when motivated to do so.
- His warmth and friendliness.
- His willingness to make eye contact and even insistence on it at times.
- The blinding brightness—*the life*—in his face and behind his eyes.

There have been no questions about any of those things on any of his evaluations, so they haven't been allowed to fight against the out-of-the-ordinary characteristics that are tallied up to reduce him to a type that most would consider forever attached to a kind of life that is certainly not fine for most of us. Data collectors and technicians don't get to see what Alex sees, nor do they seem particularly interested in anything beyond what will fit into their little boxes. They don't think he will ever be fine when every score in every category is not fine. Designations and categorizations never tell the full story.

❧

If I don't believe that he *will* be fine in at least some ways, it would be too much. The prospects and potential are the light at the end of this tunnel and they are what get me through the nights of fractured sleep and the myriad other things that remind me we are still inside it. I know one day we won't be, and I hold on to that even though I know that day might not come until we both exit this life. This is just for now. Today is only a day. Like Alex, I know that what is now is not what will always be.

❧

He will be fine by the time he is twelve, thirteen.

❧

Sometimes I look at my son and can see the man he will become underneath his sweet, still-babyish face. He is calm, he is collected, he is wise, he is loved, and most importantly, he *knows* he is loved. Whether he is twelve, thirteen, or eighty, Level 3 or no level at all, up carousing in the night or sleeping like a bear, he will always know that.

He is already fine. He will never be fine.

Everyone is fine. No one is fine.

He will be fine. He will be fine. He will be fine. He will be.

Dream #1

We are standing at an airport gate waiting to board a plane. I am holding you. You are a toddler but almost not, big but not too big to hold just yet. The terminal is crowded and loud but I am not aware of the temperature, only of yours, which feels the same as mine. Where do you end and I begin? I see your fingers, which already look like mine. The second thing I noticed the morning you were born was your hands. They were big with long fingers. I recognized you immediately. Moorer hands, Moorer eyes, which locked with mine when they put you in my arms. I am holding you at the gate waiting to board the plane. Someone is with us to help us do whatever it is we are doing, whatever it is that I am about to do that has made me have to make you go into an airport. A man, a handler, someone who is not related to us by blood or bond. He watches us carefully, ready to be ready. Airports are hard for everyone, aren't they? They are certainly hard for you—they are hard on your ears, your eyes, your skin. You are holding on to me—your arms that smell like baby powder wrapped around my neck, your legs wrapped around my waist—we must be a primitive sight and I don't care. Primitive is what we are. You and I are especially simian—I groom and feed and keep you in my sight and pull you down from trees you shouldn't climb and teach you by example—but we are not wordless on this day. On this day you say to me, "Mama, where are we going?" I tell you where. "For Mama to work some," I say. "Okay," you reply. "Baby," I say, "you're talking." Tears flow down my cheeks. You touch my face and say, "I know. I can, I just haven't been ready until now."

Sick

You are standing in the living room of your two-bedroom apartment. You hear the sound of water splashing around the corner. You pull yourself away from furiously scratching your arm while trying to comprehend an email about work to do what you know you will do—catch him with his feet in the toilet. You admittedly forget to close the lid from time to time. When you forget, he will usually, because he seems to have a sixth sense about these things, make a beeline for it, sit down on the seat backward, and joyously plop and slap his feet in the water in the bowl as if it is a puddle and he is Gene Kelly in *Singin' in the Rain*.

You round the corner and look into the bathroom. There he sits, spraying water from one end of it to the other. Normally, it's not a big deal, but today you are horrified when you see poop particles everywhere—on the toilet paper and toilet paper holder, on the floor, on the bath mat, in his hands, on his feet. You will scream whisper, yes, *scream whisper*, "How did this happen?" to no one in particular. As you put him in the bathtub to clean him up, you see that the poop you attempted to flush earlier didn't go down the toilet. You didn't notice and he doesn't care whether the water is clean or not, he just wants to play. What to do now? Autopilot. You figure he's already there and it's not that long until bath time, so you bathe him and clean up the bathroom while he soaks. You can't quite believe this has occurred, but you don't know exactly why you can't believe it. He's been home from school for twenty-five minutes. Anything can happen in twenty-five minutes. Anything can happen in *one* minute in your house.

༖

You struggled through your day already, even before he got home. You allowed H. to walk your son to school—you don't ever not walk him to school—because you felt so out of sorts you were going in circles and feared you might not have gotten him there. You were itching so violently from an allergic reaction to an antibiotic you couldn't do anything but scratch, twitch, and wish for a swift death to come upon you as quickly as possible. Misery.

You started the antibiotic last week when you were in Nashville. A thorn poked you directly in the middle of the pad above the top knuckle of the inside of your right index finger as you were putting a dozen yellow roses into a vase. Your finger began to swell shortly after the poke, but you hardly noticed and went about your day, even going to a friend's house for dinner that night. You woke up around three in the morning and discovered your finger was throbbing and about the size of one of those jumbo hot dogs you buy in an eight-pack. God, it hurt. You vowed to go to urgent care as soon as you completed the interviews that were scheduled for you to do in the morning to support the album you have coming out in four weeks. The doctor prescribed an antibiotic that turned out to be inappropriate. It was way too strong, and lo and behold you are allergic to sulfur. Who knew? You didn't. But you certainly do now.

～

Hot flashes, cold chills, goose bumps, and body aches had their way with you for two days, and then the most beautiful of all things happened—a head-to-toe rash covered you and made you wish someone would just set you on fire. You had never, ever itched so badly in your life. You fantasized about having open wounds instead of the infernal red bumps all over your body, and someone pouring bleach on you because you'd rather feel outright searing pain than this incredible gnawing that signaled something awful going on inside you. You also wanted to puke every five minutes but you didn't because you couldn't eat anything but saltines and white grapes. You were close to tears but couldn't cry any because you were also dehydrated. The doctor you finally called to come to your house this morning to the tune of eight hundred dollars told you that. "Drink more water," he said. You nodded and said you would. You got a house call because you couldn't get your regular doctor on the phone, not that he takes anything you say seriously anyway, and his staff wouldn't have gotten you in for an appointment until the late afternoon, if then, and you needed to

See.

Someone.

Right.

Away.

It was that bad. It's better now but it still hasn't passed. You got a cortisone shot from the house-call doctor that felt like the fire you wished for but only in a concentrated spot in your left upper butt cheek. You passed out for seventy-five minutes after the doctor left because you hardly slept at all last night because of the tossing, turning, and scratching. You tried not to worry about the money you just spent on thirty minutes, a shot, and two prescriptions. You ignored text messages and phone calls from those concerned about you. You pulled yourself out of bed at the very last minute you could because you needed to get your prescriptions for anti-itch medicine and more steroids filled, then get back home in time to feed and walk the dog, then go pick up your son from school.

Your son screamed at you when you crouched down to tell him hello at school pickup. You apologized for not walking him to school that morning but reminded him you were there now. He seemed satisfied, took your hand, and you walked home together. You made it inside the building before he kicked off both of his sandals. You picked them up and carried them while herding him into the elevator. You unbuckled the strap on his backpack while you rode the four floors up just as you always do, taking it up in your own arms so that he was unencumbered as quickly as possible and was happier. You tried to keep everything consistent even though there was nothing consistent about you. But that's what you do, isn't it? No matter if you want to claw your face off. No matter if you're dry-heaving. No matter if you're brokenhearted. No matter what, you do. You do, no matter what. There is no indignity too undignified; you are where the buck stops. You clean up the poop and the puke, even when you think you won't be able. There is no space to be carved out and marked as private—not your bed, your bathroom time, not your sick days, or even your dinner plate. You share it all. It can be a little much some days. But mostly, especially on those Saturday mornings when everyone is feeling better—the itch has stopped, you remembered to close the toilet lid, and everyone has eaten a little bit of breakfast—you will look over at him sitting beside you on the couch and only be thankful you were given the blessing of guiding him, however unsteadily, through the world. You are reading the paper while he calmly listens to music on his iPad. You can breathe. Then he reaches over, with typical rattlesnake-like speed, and dunks his hand in your coffee. You patiently take his hand out of the mug, get up off the sofa and carry it to the kitchen, pour the coffee out, and tell yourself you don't need any more caffeine as you spy a perfectly curlicued dog turd to the right of the dining table. You reach for the paper towels.

The Wormhole

Shit. Will I have a bruise? I have a lunch meeting to-morrow. I stare at myself in the bathroom mirror while I wipe away the bulbous tears falling down my face. It was just Mucinex, damn it.

It hurts to touch the bone that holds up my left eye-brow. That's where he got me. A headbutt. I swear some-times that there are things about my face that are different from the way they were before this happened. The shifts probably aren't all due to age. I exhale slowly, heavily, exhaustedly.

                      ~

I gave him increasing amounts of Skittles to reward him for every drop he allowed down his throat. One for the first milliliter, two for the next two, three for three, un-til he got to eight milliliters (the proper dose is ten) then lost his temper. I'd gotten him early from school. He has a cold. I can predict what he will do a lot of the time but he's quick. I didn't see this one coming. What a thing, to brace yourself against your child, to learn to try to block the blows you know might come.

It feels awful to have to. It's confusing. How do I protect him and myself all at the same time? What a mind fuck. We're told to get away from those who hurt us, but I can't, nor do I want to, run away from this person, my child, who sometimes lashes out at me. I also can't help my physical reaction to threat, which is thankfully limited to raising my arms to block his, ducking my head, or holding his wrists when his fingers become so tightly wound in my hair I think there's no way I can prevent him from ripping it all out by the roots.

He isn't lashing out because he means to harm me or because he can help it; he's angry and frustrated and can't say so. He has no other way to express his dissatisfaction or his pain. Some moments can feel like we're in a bubble of frustration together—one we can't get out of and no one else can come into. His frustration: Unspoken and only physically demonstrated save for the sounds he makes that don't form words, not ones I can understand anyway. He cries and throws his head into the pillow on his bed while screaming or he gets aggressive. My frustration: Bewildered and discombobulated, and only finally shown when I feel beaten, usually through bawling my head off or asking God through my sobs to please help us when I'm unable not to take it personally anymore, when I feel like he must hate me to hurt me, when I stare down the barrel of this beast, fast-forward eight or so years, and see him as a person much larger and stronger than I am still being violent with me because he can't express himself. What will I do then?

⌒

It's my fault. I shouldn't have had him sitting on the pass-through so he would be eye level with me while I gave him the medicine. I needed him not to be able to run from me. Is there a way I could've done it better? I've tried basically sitting on him and holding his mouth open and pouring medicine down his throat. That scares him to death and he spits it out anyway and I certainly don't like to get physical any more than I like it when he gets physical with me. I can just barely control him anyway. In fact, I can't anymore—the barely has now been replaced by an increase in his strength and will and a decline in mine. Surely other mamas don't have this problem. Maria probably gets Brian to take medicine like it's grape Kool-Aid. Why is everyone better at this than I am?

⌒

Okay, okay. He is sick. If I couldn't tell my mama my head felt like it was about to split open, I might have head-butted her too. It's possible that she'd have responded by knocking me into next week if I had. I do no such thing, but that isn't necessarily easy every time. I think about how angry I become when he does it. I think about how tenuous self-control really is. I think about the differences between one person's breaking point and another's. I think about how grateful I am for the special patience I must reserve for this set of circumstances and how it is, without a doubt, sent from a higher power. I think about how I cannot understand physical abuse against children or against anyone. I think about how it is a miracle that I can't, given my own childhood.

∽

I often say that I think he knows everything, but if he does, then he knows that he hurts me, and if he knows that, then how can he do it, and if he can do it, then how can he know? He doesn't know. He knows but he can't help it. Something that I don't understand takes over his mind or his impulsivity charges in and reacting physically is his only available reaction. If he laughs, it's because he's responding to my anguished facial expression, right? I'm sure I look a fright. That he laughs must mean he doesn't understand, he doesn't know. That he laughs must mean he feels safe. That is a bright side to these realizations. Or maybe what he'd like to do is cry but his brain sends the wrong signal to his body. If I think about it too much, I despair too much. That's not good for either one of us.

The circular thinking. The wormhole. The whole thing twists in my mind like an automobile twisting around a tree during an accident, sounds included. I worry about the wreckage.

❦

I sometimes don't like to think about what could lie ahead if we're not careful every single day of our lives. There's enough history of violence in my life to keep flashing lights and middle-of-the-night phone calls readily imaginable. What do I do if he attacks someone else? What do I do if he does it and he's not in a structured, controlled environment? Who will explain if there's no one there who understands? Who will protect him from those who need protection from him? I don't need to list the possible horrifying scenarios.

This morning I had to separate him from a teacher at drop-off. I was headed toward the front door of the school to return home when he shoved his fingers into her hair, pulled her head down, and tried to bite her face. I heard the commotion, pivoted, crouched down in front of him, and took his wrists in my hands just as I have to do when he applies a death grip to my stringy strands. I calmly told him that he would let go and that what he'd done wasn't acceptable. He must've been feeling bad already from the cold that is now apparent. I didn't catch it.

They don't like it when a parent steps in at school. Ignore it, they say. If you give it attention, it only reinforces it, they tell us. Well, that may be true, but easier said than done. Could they stay calm if their child was in distress and could only let someone know about it by being physically aggressive? I can almost handle it most of the time when he does it to me, but I cannot abide my child taking out his frustration on another. I'll stay in the bubble with him. So be it.

The agonizing worry. The fear. The wormhole. The dark thoughts I'm not supposed to admit. Isn't it good that I can admit them? I think there would be much more cause for worry if I didn't say them, or at least write them, out loud. I think, multiple times per day, about who will fend for him if his dad or I can't, about how much he needs me no matter what the circumstances are, about how I want to fight for him and not with him, about how very much I love him, about how I might love him most of all during these moments. I shake myself out of the emotional brownout, look at my watch, and calculate when he needs his next dose.

Grace Note

Dear Neighbor,

I understand that you are frustrated with the sounds you hear coming from our apartment on the floor above you. My six-year-old son, John Henry, has nonverbal autism and is often up in the night. He also likes to jump up and down. He has a trampoline in his room that he is encouraged to and does use, but that doesn't stop him from jumping off of furniture, or just jumping in general, when he becomes excited or has the need for sensory stimulation. I apologize for his disturbing you. I have received your complaints through the building management, and explained that, yes, we do have rugs down when it was suggested that we didn't, and there's only so much I can do about the issue. I know it's not a great situation. I wish I could change it not only for you, but also for me, and mostly for him. I do so regret, however, that it causes those around us such discomfort. It would cause him sadness to know he is contributing to your unhappiness.

However, your banging on your ceiling does nothing but exacerbate the problem and causes us much more stress than there would be if I could try to calm him without the added pressure of your shouting and striking our floor. I would appreciate it if, the next time you are shaken from your slumber, your work, or daily activities, you would refrain from such behavior.

If you would like, please come up for a cup of tea or coffee and we can discuss the issue as neighbors instead of enemies. You might also like to meet the six-year-old with extreme sensory issues that you consider such a menace to your peace.

Sincerely,
Allison Moorer, 4A

∾

Grace note: An extra note added as an embellishment and not essential to the harmony or the melody.

∾

Dear Woman in the Yes-I-Know-It's-a-Women's-Locker-Room,

I heard you say "Don't bring boys in here" and I heard you brush off my attempt to explain with "I don't care! He's too big!" I heard you tell me "I told the lifeguard to tell you to use the family locker room. She should've told you to do that. People can't bring boys in here with naked women." I'm sorry you didn't seem to hear my apology or maybe it just didn't matter to you. I had no idea there was a family locker room. I kept my son—his name is John Henry—facing the wall even though you were on the other side of a wall of lockers. He was quiet. He looked embarrassed. We got dressed. I could hear you muttering. I'm sorry you refused to listen to me that day so I'd like to try to explain again. John Henry was with me because he has autism and is nonverbal. I'm sorry I can't let him loose in the men's locker room where he has no idea what to do or how to get out of his swimsuit and into dry clothes on his own, and I'm sorry I can't let him wait for me outside because he might wander back into the pool by himself. He might drown.

I would also like you to know that I later apologized to John Henry first for myself, because I know I should've just ignored you and let you spin out alone. But I apologized for you too, because you too are a human being.

Sincerely,
Scared Mother That
You Shouted At in
the Yes-I-Know-
It's-a-Women's-
Locker-Room

∼

Dear Leelee,

Remember that day you bought us both the tie-on bracelets with the five Guatemalan worry dolls on them? The dolls that you're supposed to rub when you're worried over something out of your control? Remember how we doubled over with laughter when we saw that three of the dolls on my bracelet had fallen off by the end of the day and we decided they'd jumped, that they realized they couldn't help me? Thank you for laughing with me and for making me feel like I'm not alone in my mama-worrying. Thank you for getting it.

Love,
Lala

∽

Grace starts within. This might be the grace note I need most of all.

Dear Allison,

You, almost all of the time, do the best that you can.

You, almost all of your life, have done the best that you can.

You, a few times, have been dealt some cards that made bad hands. You, almost every time, played them the best that you knew how.

You, almost never, are expected by anyone else to be perfect, so please give yourself a break and stop expecting perfection from yourself. If you can learn to do that, you will stop expecting so much from others and all of this living will be a little easier.

You, almost always, can let go a little bit more than is your nature to do. Try to relearn how tight your grip should be. Loosen your hands a little now.

You, every day, are tougher than you think you are and more fragile than you let on.

You, every time it happens, need to listen when someone tells you that you're doing a good job. Those are not hollow words.

You have not ever been, and are not now, in a race. There is no finish line in life. What are you going to do when you get it all done? You will do some more. There will never be a time when you will be done. You will just have to stop one day. Remember to remember to enjoy it while you can still think a clear thought and say a prayer of thankfulness for the life, bulging with blessings, that you have lived and still get to live.

You, on so many occasions that you are aware of and even more that you are not, have been afforded masses of grace. You have no idea how close to death you have been on so very many occasions and yet you are still here, mostly in one piece. You are still here—here to live this beautiful life, here to live up to the honor of raising this child you love so much, here to be uniquely you. Trust that it will work out okay because at this point, don't you think it will? Try doing that the best that you can now. Screw the rest.

Love,
Allison

Snow Day

I take my first sip of coffee as I sit cross-legged in my reading spot on the sofa. I listen for sounds from his room. It's 8:34 a.m. on a Thursday.

"This is different," I say to myself. How nice. I looked in on him when I made my way down the hallway after I woke, but his eyes were still closed. A miracle, I thought. He hardly ever sleeps past seven. Maybe he slept as deeply as I did—as if the snowfall had made a heavy, velvet blanket and tenderly held me down, allowing me a sort of sleep that is usually inaccessible.

Maybe it's that I let him stay up late last night. The group text chain with some of the other mothers from his school started buzzing around six thirty p.m. yesterday with the news that public schools would be closed today, therefore *our* school would be closed today. We don't take such news lightly. No parent does, I know, as we all have to quickly shuffle to make accommodations for our children who suddenly have nowhere to be, but my fellow autism mothers and I especially don't. Our children present some unique challenges when they're off of their routines and inside at home all day. Part of school for us is constant supervision for them. Left alone, my son can break a piece of furniture, do a startlingly good impression of Mumble from *Happy Feet* while standing up in the bathtub or toilet, or decorate the living room with the sliced mango he would've secretly extracted from the refrigerator quicker than I can brush my teeth.

I tried to take the news of the snow day in stride. I genuinely like my son, and enjoy his company most of the time despite his ability to wreck the whole apartment in a flash, so I sort of looked forward to spending a cozy day inside after I gave up looking for a flight to get us out of New York City and to somewhere possibly warmer and with more space. Yes, I did do a panicked search for flights to Miami—could we get somewhere where swimming for three days might be an option?—and even to Tennessee—a fenced yard would work too—and was willing to make my credit card groan to buy them. It was possible that schools might be closed on Friday as well and we would've made a long weekend out of it, but every flight out was already canceled. These walls, fortunate as we are to have them, can feel quite thick and isolating, especially in winter. Some days I feel like we're stuck in a parallel universe that no one else sees or understands—one where it isn't unusual for a child to want to take five or six baths a day, or ask for over a dozen Popsicles in a four-hour period. The other mothers on the group text understand. But even we have our particular and peculiar sets of circumstances. Some of our children are fully self-sufficient in self-care, some aren't. Some have verbal abilities, some only communicate through echolalia, and some have no words at all, like mine, and we are left with iPads and sign language to try to communicate. Some, like mine, are flexible about changing environments and schedules, but some are thrown completely off by travel and time zones and even weekends. All of our babies require extra patience and the deepest sort of love and understanding. Most of them get exactly that.

I'm lucky. My boy is good-natured and happy and goes with the flow most of the time. But it's January in New York City. He isn't above getting frustrated and throwing a fit when he has to be inside all day long. He doesn't necessarily understand that bad weather makes it dangerous to go out for a walk or to the park, or he doesn't care. The winter days can be, despite the absence of the sun, intolerably long. We do what we have to, to get through them—we take as many baths, eat as many Popsicles, and watch as many movies as we need to.

⌒

The clock now shows 9:00 a.m. *Unbelievable*, I think. He never sleeps this late and it actually worries me a little. Is he sick? I go to his bedroom, crouch down by his bed, and see that his eyes are open. He starts to hum the tune he was singing yesterday when I was drying him off after his bath. He gives me the sweetest smile and puts his arms around my neck, pulling me toward him for a hug. I tell him good morning and inhale as my nose sinks into his head of thick blond hair that's just like my mama's. These are the moments that I wait on, when I can actually *feel* instead of just have faith that he loves me, when I sense that he is at peace, when his mood is happy, content, and there is an aura of safety around us.

I point to the window and remind him that he doesn't have school today because of the snow, then leave him to lounge after I tell him to take as long as he wants to get up, that we've got nowhere to go and nothing to do but snuggle in. I go to the kitchen and start cooking bacon, currently his favorite food in the world. I pop open a can of cinnamon rolls and put them in the oven while I talk to H. about what we'd like to get done today despite our routines having gone out the same window I just pointed to in the boy's room. I wonder if this is what it's like in other families. It's quiet, even calm in the apartment.

I put the bacon on a plate I'd covered with paper towels. I spread the icing on the hot cinnamon rolls. I placed one on a plate and cut it up into bite-sized pieces for John Henry, who has made his way to his chair and is sipping the glass of milk I'd set on his beloved, faded robot placemat. I put the plate down in front of him. He looks up and smiles at me as he reaches for the bacon I've placed in the middle of the table for all of us to share. *Is the barometric pressure having some effect on his mood?* I silently wonder. I

64

start going through the reasons that he might be at ease so I can remember them when he is not—rain usually makes him dark and susceptible to crying jags, and isn't snow just frozen rain? Maybe he had a good dream. Maybe he's just like any other kid and he's happy he doesn't have to go to school today. Like in other families . . .

⌒

My preoccupation with autism makes me see him as an autistic boy too often. I know he has typical wants and needs—he wants to go outside and play, he wants to run and jump and holler, he wants to watch movies, he likes dogs, he loves music, he likes to sleep in his mama's bed when he's sick or if he's been away at his dad's house— but could it be that the scale is tipping today? As I learn to live with his challenges, could it be that he is as well? Thinking about what he has to overcome makes my heart hurt, and thinking about him giving his best effort makes it hurt worse—my sweet boy—I wish he had it easier. I think about what he must think about. I think about what he must have to process, what hurdles he has to clear in order to communicate even the smallest thing. He has to figure out how to say it all without saying it. So much is missed with such an imperfect system. So much is lost. No wonder he seems impulsive sometimes. He may not actually be more impulsive than anyone else by nature; he may just run out of the vast supply of persistence that's required to go through all of the steps it must take for him to not grab something he wants to eat off of a plate, whether it's his or not. I think about how remarkable he is and how he stops to request most of the things he wants and needs with the limited sign language to which he has access. I think about how I would lose my patience and how I wouldn't have any strength to throw my arms around my mama and smile if I had to get through what he does. I am humbled by his presence and his grace.

❧

He has two bathroom accidents in the morning. I hardly blink an eye. I habitually run through the list of possible digestion-disrupting culprits but I don't drown in the thoughts, I don't agonize; I let them come and go and almost lightheartedly think to myself that we'll figure it out someday, when he is ready. I say a silent prayer that he will indeed be ready soon. He plays with his iPad in his room, humming along to the music or along with nothing at all that I can hear while I answer emails and figure out when I can carve some writing time into this day. I cross my fingers in my mind. *Please don't let him have a meltdown. Please let him stay happy. Please let us get through this day without tears.*

He runs down the battery in the iPad. I plug it in to charge and start a movie on the television. I leave him sitting on the sofa with H. while I sneak away to drop off laundry and go to the gym for a quick workout. I walk back in the door forty-five minutes later and they're where I left them. The bathroom timer has thirteen minutes left on it—phew, I made it. He's still happy. Nothing is wrecked.

I sit down beside him on the sofa as he pushes the small Moroccan-style table that sits in front of it over with his foot. It falls apart. Oh well. It is 4:57 p.m., I've written 1,136 words, I've answered emails, we are fed, I've exercised, he is clean, he is happy. I am thankful for this snow day. I am thankful for every day, but especially those that erect scaffolding around hope.

〜

4:59 p.m. The bathroom timer sounds and I stand up, tell him it's time to go to the bathroom, take his hand, and walk him there. He stands by the toilet and sticks his left foot into the corner of the tiled room—he's always looking for even a miniscule amount of water to splash in. There isn't any in the corner today; it's just his habit to check. I make the sign for *bathroom*—fingers down over my palm and the thumb sticking up through my index and middle fingers. He makes it too. He goes to the bathroom, then gets up, stands there, and wraps his arms around my neck, underwear and pants still down around his ankles. I pat his back and tell him to pull up his pants. He screams loudly into my ear while wringing his hands. My eardrum rattles. Here it comes, I think. I take my chances and tell him to pull up his pants again. He does and smiles without another sound.

Dream #2

We are riding in the back of a pickup truck. We are in Frankville, Alabama, where I lived until I was twelve years old. I always thought I would feel at home on New York City streets as I learned how to navigate them but I didn't—it is these dirt paths that I still know like they were etched on the inside of my skin, on the inside of my eyelids. How could anywhere but here ever be home? You are home with me. We are sitting on the wheel wells across from each other, the same way I used to do when I was a girl. I am older now but the pasture roads haven't changed. I feel where they are still muddy, sandy, gravelly as the tires send the signals to my vibrating bones. Your great-grandfather, my Dandy, is driving, inching along the way he does when he's checking on cows and things. He holds a Salem menthol out the rolled-down window and smoke wafts into my nose. He has known you your entire life and thinks you're a fine boy. He's especially proud when you wear the denim overalls you're wearing today. He died six years before you were born. We are in time and out of time. The sunshine hits your hair and it looks like gold. You squint your eyes as you look up to the sky. You are ageless. You are five years old. We drive away from Dry Creek and back toward Dandy's barn, passing the big old oak tree in the middle of the pasture. You say to me, "Look at that tree, Mama. It has so much moss hanging on it! I like it. I like it here." You are home with me. You are home to me.

Awe

I watched the video your teacher took
Downright brilliant, I said
Rhythm you found inside the sounds
Escaping from squeaky gears
At the playground
Monday afternoon
You locked into it
Ooo-doo-doo-doo Doo-doo-doo Doo-doo-
    doo Ooo-doo-doo-doo Doo-doo-doo
    Doo-doo-doo
Unbelievably cool, staggeringly smart
Tell me too many times
About what you hear running through that mind
    of yours
Let the world
Know your inscape

The symphonic supercalifragilisticexpialidocious
Only you hear
Measureless is your melody
Eternal and sonorous is your voice

Ho Ho Hum

The writing wouldn't come that morning, so I reached for one of the catalogs that had been pushed into our mailbox that week and flipped through it while I sat list-lessly at my desk. I kept a stack of the ones with toys in them thinking I might find something. John Henry was still asleep in his bedroom around the corner and the morning light, what little there was on that December day, had not yet slipped through his bedroom window.

Toys. Christmas. Santa Claus. Elves. Oh yes, I remem-bered, this is how it's supposed to go. These are the things I'm supposed to buy. These are the things the neurotypical children think about and this is the world in which we don't really live.

Visions of sugarplums. I wondered, what vision of Christmas does my son have? Does he comprehend the talking he hears about chimneys and presents and naughty and nice and bad and good? Does he look forward to it or is it just another day?

Another thing about which I have absolutely no idea. I have my suspicions—when I mention Santa sometimes I get a little smile out of him—but he doesn't have any issues going to sleep on Christmas Eve like I did when I was little. He doesn't ask me to put out milk and cookies, nor does he wake up earlier on Christmas morning than on any other. He writes no letter requesting this or that wish to be granted, and he makes no list of toys that he would like. If he knows, maybe it's just not a big deal to him. If he knows, maybe I'm missing the clues that he cares.

I hate it when I miss the clues.

∽

His first Christmas was what I imagine most privileged children's first Christmases are like. I bought way too many toys—a little red piano with eighteen keys, gadgets that played music when prompted, toy trains, trucks, books, stuffed animals—and put them all around the tree on Christmas Eve. It was way too much, but it was what I thought I was supposed to do. On that Christmas morning, he registered as much excitement as an eight-month-old can, but mostly played the little red Schoenhut piano and la-la-la'd along in his sweet baby voice. We were delighted that he gravitated toward the piano—immediately pronouncing he'd be a player, of course. We had already decided he'd be *some* sort of entertainer as he'd not only *not* cried in his first photo with Santa a few days earlier but went so far as to wave at the camera. He spent a lot of his first year waving at people and, as soon as he could, saying "Hey" to them. It was the cutest thing I'd ever seen.

The next Christmas was different. I knew something was wrong but exactly what hadn't been confirmed. We were still in the watch-and-wait stage, though I knew that the sweet infant who waved and said "Hey" to cameras and people on airplanes had gone away somewhere. I couldn't get him to come back. I knew he might not ever, though I wouldn't admit it and—frustratingly, for myself and I'm sure for him—kept trying to draw him back out.

That I might not ever again see that engaged and social boy who made eye contact with strangers didn't stop the world from turning or Christmas from coming. The instructions to be merry and bright didn't wait until we adjusted to a new normal, one that didn't include a growing list of words he could say. If anything, time seemed to speed up even as I prayed for more of it to put between a strange developmental phase and profound autism. We bought more toys his second Christmas, but John Henry had narrowed his focus to the details—the switch that he could toggle on and off on this behemoth of plastic that made jungle noises, the wheels of that car that he could spin with his hands. I watched with a mixture of astonishment, despair, and stubborn belief that he, and we, could somehow change his trajectory. I hung on to the notion that he, and we, would become typical again, something like average one day, some sort of appropriately excited about it all some year.

～

The following spring brought the diagnosis, but I kept on with the overload of presents when December rolled around again, hoping to happen upon something for Santa to bring that John Henry would like or even react to. Scooters, balls, stuffed animals, books, crayons and coloring books, paint sets. I was trying to reach him. For several years, in fact, I gathered my enthusiasm each Christmas Eve as I set everything out for him to find the following morning, thinking there had to be something that would catch his interest. I never found it, though I would've led a pony into our living room if I'd thought it would've made a difference.

～

I thumbed through the catalog and stopped on page twenty.

Koala Crate is inspired by the way kids learn—through play! Each month explores a new, preschool-perfect theme like Farms, Rainbows, Transportation, or Reptiles. Inside each crate you'll find all the creative materials you need for multiple hands-on activities, a parent instruction guide, and our *Imagine!* magazine created especially for kids. Koala Crate makes it convenient—and a joy—for these budding innovators and their grownup assistants to spend time building and learning together. Starts at $16.95/month.

The Koala Crate sounded super cool. A few years ago I probably would've tried it out and spent the $16.95 per month hoping that I could inspire him to play with me, to sit and pursue an activity that might open him up, or at the very least allow him some fun for a little while. I know better now. Wikki Stix aren't used to build but are rather chewed on or thrown to the floor by the handful. The rickrack and tissue paper in the photos—well, those would go straight into his mouth, along with the buttons for making eyes and noses for any dreamed-up animal and the construction paper included for practicing scissor skills. John Henry still has to be prompted to make snips in paper. That skill has been on his occupational therapy goals list for years. He doesn't take to it. Why bother using scissors? Teeth are much more efficient and they are always accessible. Hands need to be used for other things.

I moved on. Page twenty-two.

Tadpole Crate. Share the joy of discovery with your youngest explorer! Created in collaboration with experts at Seattle Children's Hospital, Tadpole Crate fosters healthy development at every stage. Each month, you'll receive age-appropriate projects to support developmental milestones, plus a magazine that explains how the projects benefit your little one. (Did you know that sorting sea creatures promotes crucial logic and reasoning skills?) Starts at $16.95/month.

John Henry can sort sea creatures. In fact, he spends a lot of time sorting things at school. He's been sorting since he was two. He doesn't want to sort at home. He's as sick of sorting as I am of making him do it. But sorting promotes logic and reasoning skills. Okay. Maybe sorting is what has enabled him to bring me the shoes he wears to the pool when he wants to go swimming. He has to pick out the right pair from the row of them that sits just underneath his bed. But does the fact that he doesn't care about sorting mean he is developmentally somewhere between zero and two years old? Does the fact that he has to sort things at school suggest that? No. It doesn't. John Henry can do many things that are age appropriate and beyond but it appears that he just doesn't care to sort for the sake of sorting, so he doesn't do it on his own. Never would it cross his mind, it seems, to put things into categories that make sense to others. We sort, as human beings. We make piles of things, categorize colors and shapes and animals and even (mostly, sometimes) people, but John Henry apparently has no use for that. He's not the type of autistic who lines his toys up in a row and separates them by color. He's the type to throw them all onto the floor and dance around the pile because the noise makes him excited. He may never excel at putting things in an order, but I have to look at the blessing in that and envy his natural rejection of the idea that everything can be categorized. Those who would suggest his cognitive inferiority might want to consider his spiritual advancement.

I moved on again. Page twenty-eight.

Fan Faves! Here's a selection of a few of our customer favorites. Pinball Machine $24.95. Explore angles, momentum, and geometric art while designing a playable pinball machine. Speedy Race Cars $15.95. Create and customize two race cars, and a speedway for them to zoom across! Chalkboard & Glow Slime $22.95. It's slime time! Make chalkboard slime you can scribble on, and slime that glows in the dark. Fire Lab $34.95. Conduct seven experiments exploring the chemistry of combustion and oxidation. Chomping Mechanical Dinosaur Costume $29.95.

I know of children on the spectrum who would revel in building and experimenting and imaginative play, but we're not there yet. This many years after that second Christmas when I first knew, and I can finally say we may never be there without it totally derailing my day. I was not about to let those catalogs derail my day either. I almost picked up the next one in the stack, but instead stood up from my desk and took them all to the trash can.

❧

I thought of my own childhood. Scrawled letters to Santa asking for a baby doll or Mickey Mouse wristwatch, a maroon banana-seat bicycle for me and a ten-speed for my sister when I was in second grade, by that time singing a solo in the school Christmas pageant every year. Getting up on Christmas morning before my parents and running down the hallway to their bedroom door to shout, "Come look what Santa Claus brought!" John Henry can't yet write his name. I've tried to get him to wear a watch so he might be able to learn to tell time but he resists anything like that and pulls it off immediately. He will only ride a bicycle for four or five feet before he loses interest. He can sing, but only what he wants to.

I remembered comparison is the enemy of happiness. I remembered we project our childhoods onto our children's if we aren't very careful. I remembered that I remember very few peaceful childhood Christmases. I reminded myself that my son's are not like mine. I was grateful that they are not.

I also remembered that I've at least somewhat dreaded the holiday season for years now. I wish I didn't, know I shouldn't, and that whether or not I can figure out what Santa Claus can bring John Henry should not be the point. I know that I should make the best of it and enjoy it, to maybe even get some comfort out of his disinterest in material goods, but that we don't have a typical experience stings during the holiday season more than the rest of the year. By the time Thanksgiving rolls around I can't help but worry that I'm letting him miss out on something. I worry that he wants things he can't tell me about.

I hate it when I miss the clues. What if there are clues?

⁓

I've almost lost track of what it's like for typical children. I almost can't remember what it's *supposed* to be like for them. What do typical eight-year-old boys even like? I researched.

A robot kit.

A Nerf bow.

A Nerf blaster.

Lego kits.

Jenga.

Things to build things with, things to shoot things with.

Hmmm. John Henry has to be coerced to use glue properly and not taste it. They work on that at school. He puts the pieces of anything that must be put together in his mouth, and as far as I know has no knowledge of weapons other than his own hands or teeth.

If I buy him some sort of toy or kit, he'll show a bit of interest, but if he cannot figure out what to do with it immediately, he'll lose that interest and walk away. Attempts to redirect him back to it are met with frustration and tears, as if he knows I want him to do something, to perform the way he's expected to do at school all day, and he doesn't want to. Or he can't. I don't have the energy or heart to ABA a toy with him like I'm supposed to, to enable him to learn how to play in a step-by-step fashion like they do at school. Doing so would feel like schoolwork to him *and* to me and he is beyond unenthusiastic about such methods being used at home. What's the point if it's meaningless to him? I don't have the heart to make him do anything so that I can try to fool myself into thinking that he's not that far removed from the neurotypical children like I used to. Those days are long gone.

I don't suppose we do much of anything the supposed normal way. Leelee reminds me that normal is a setting on the dryer, but her son plays football and is on the archery team at school and just got his driver's license. Meanwhile, I don't let go of John Henry's hand when we're walking somewhere for fear that he'll run away or into the street. He isn't on any sports teams. He doesn't even tell me which shirt he'd like to wear if I give him a choice between two. Sometimes he'll point at one instead of the other if I remember to ask him to during the sometimes stressful activity that is getting dressed, but I have no real indication of his favorite color, though I think it might be blue because when there's a blue choice he usually goes with it, especially if there's a dinosaur theme. We don't talk about school or his friends. We don't have playdates. I try to concentrate on the things that I know he does like. It's not as if I'm not paying attention, even if I do miss clues.

∼

On Christmas Eve, H. and I blew up red, yellow, green, blue, purple, and pink balloons stamped with Trolls faces until we could barely breathe and stuck them into the holes that ran up the corporate business balloon tree I'd found on Amazon.com. Balloons are John Henry's obsession at the moment. Surely he will like this, I thought. I scattered the fidget toys, squirmy plastic worms, and squishy plastic balls that I bought in bulk across a wooden tray that I put on the sofa. I tried to make it all look as Christmas-y as I could, and I smiled and shook my head a little at the uniqueness of such a display. I stood and looked at it all before I turned out the lights. A balloon fell off the tree and bounced a few times then stopped, but I didn't move to put it back on. I just fought back the mixture of happy and sad tears that welled up in my eyes and went to bed, setting my clock for 6 a.m. so I would wake before he did. I wanted to be waiting for him, so I could direct him to his squishy toys and balloon tree, so he might get excited about what Santa had left, so he might know how much he is loved, so Christmas might not be just another day, at least for a minute.

⌒

Our home was warm. I'd put up the tree and decorated it with the pretty and the sentimental ornaments, including the ones that John Henry has made at school since he was just a tiny boy. One thing he does seem to appreciate is the festive decor. He'll sit and stare at the lights on the tree or jiggle a particular ornament back and forth whenever it catches his eye. He'll also remove one while I'm not looking if he likes it enough and I'll never see it again until it's beyond repair—a few years ago he bit the heads off of four glorious, glittery, feathered birds that I bought in blue and purple, Ozzy Osbourne style. Maybe he'll be a performer after all. Did I mention laughter is a requirement for getting through this season? For getting through this life?

I'd hung the garland and the wreaths. I'd planned the menus for morning, noon, and night. I'd made everything the way I thought it was supposed to be. There were cakes and cookies—I did it all the way I've always dreamed it and even raised the bar a little. But what I cannot pull off, what I cannot do, is make my son play the role in all of this that I thought he would. He has no interest in the way things are supposed to be, and I get it. But I do. I'm supposed to be able to give him a Christmas that is not just like any other day. I fear that I'm not achieving that. I fear that nothing I do can make it so.

❧

I got up the next morning and made coffee. I put pans of cinnamon rolls and sausage rolls into the oven. John Henry rose around seven thirty and immediately headed toward the back door. He wanted to go outside just like he does every morning. Either he forgot what I told him about Santa or he wasn't that interested in what magic might've been waiting for him in the living room. I directed him away from the window and toward the balloon tree on the other end of the house.

He saw it and within five minutes there were balloons everywhere. He pulled them from the balloon tree, tossed them, beat on them with his hands, and kicked them about. To my delight, he noticed there were Trolls on them. A success! We listened to music, he kicked balloons, he grabbed handfuls of squishy toys and threw them to the floor, then picked them back up again to jiggle them. He didn't bring them to me for me to see, but he seemed happy and even excited for a minute. He then charged into the breakfast room and stopped to take a bite of a cinnamon roll before he tapped on the glass of the back door to tell me he wanted to go outside. I laughed, sighed, turned him around, and pointed him back toward his bedroom to get him bundled up for the weather. It might've been just like any other day, but good ones are always like Christmas to me.

The Breath

The caller ID said "Spring OB/GYN."

"Mammogram," I barely whispered to the heavy air that hung in between my lips and the screen that gave me a choice to answer, decline, or send the call to voicemail.

I'd had the procedure just the day before. They don't call unless there's a reason. A shiver rolled across my shoulders and down my spine, then I exhaled, remembering that morning's meditation about always returning to the breath.

"Hello?"

"Hi, Allison. It's Dr. Smith calling about your results from yesterday. You have a lesion in the right breast as well as a cluster of cysts—you need to go back in and have a targeted ultrasound. I'm going to send over the referral to the radiology office right now. Then you'll need to go back in six months for another general ultrasound on both breasts to monitor the cysts."

"Okay. I had a feeling I'd be doing this. My right one is the problem sister of the two."

"Oh, haha! Yes, they can be that way, can't they? I'm sure it's all fine, we just like to be extra cautious, as you know."

Yes, I knew. I'd been through this once already, only two years ago, when there was something suspicious discovered in my right breast for the first time. MY right breast, not THE right breast, as she called it. A depersonalization technique, I assume. Maybe I'll start referring to my breasts as THE breasts, and not MY breasts. Maybe that will help me divorce myself from them, to treat them like some separate things—two pouches of adipose tissue, lobes, blood vessels, lymph nodes, and, in my case, lesions and cysts that sit on my chest and will likely turn to rot—some visitors only temporarily attached to me. Maybe then if MY breasts, THE breasts, must be DEtached I won't notice or care so much. I will not see them as ever having been a part of me, and might even be glad they're finally gone, like the last party guests who didn't pick up on the cue to leave and have begun to appear a bit bedraggled.

I could imagine them gone. I remember taking curious peeks at my grandmother's flat chest through the loose armholes of the sleeveless summer tops she'd wear around the house and yard to do chores. She'd usually forgo putting on the suffocating bra that held the hard, pointy prosthetic breasts when she was at home. I got the best glimpses when she'd lift her arms to hang laundry on the clothesline. The skin on her chest was white but looked scarred, as if she'd been burned. I didn't understand what had happened, only that her chest looked nothing like my mama's. Mammy didn't talk about it. No one did.

I've always had a sense that something was unstable about my right breast and I've prepared myself for this sort of news. I began having mammograms at thirty-five instead of waiting until the recommended age of forty for exactly that reason. So I'm ready for this, right? Wrong. Even though I'd gotten the feeling that this would be the year as I lay on the chair/table in the dark radiology office the day before—I'd heard too many beeps from the machine, I thought it was taking way too much time—I didn't know if I could trust that little voice in my head that whispered this might be the year. I didn't have any signs, save for the cyclical tenderness and knottiness. I can't consider my general fatigue. I'm not well rested enough to do that. I can't consider my lack of appetite. I'm not consistently anxiety-free enough to do that.

I called the radiology office and made an appointment. Then I called the people with whom I'm supposed to share things like news of breast lesions and clusters of cysts. My sister, my best friend Leelee, and H. I hated doing it, but I would want to know if their problem sister was throwing a tantrum again and what was going to be done to remedy her fit. Sissy told me not to worry and said it would all be fine, that I just needed yet another thing to fret over and the universe had provided. Ashley said she didn't want me to have to wait that long for an appointment and asked if I couldn't get it done somewhere else sooner. I said no, and I was busy anyway so it would work out. H. took a deep breath and started talking about what to do—should I just have them removed? I said I was considering it. We had a bad connection. He was somewhere on the road in Texas and I told him we could talk about it later if he wanted but that it was very likely going to turn out to be nothing. He knew as much as I did anyway. He'd sat with me in the office of the doctor who told me my cancer odds two years ago when I had the first scare. He'd cried after she said that I was all right for the moment, but I didn't. I instead focused on having, according to her, about a 30 percent chance of developing it based on family history and dense breast tissue alone. She encouraged genetic testing, which I still haven't had. I'm not sure how it would help me deal with something that is so likely to occur. There is no vaccination against this interloper that waits around the corner. All I can do is watch for signs of another brutal beast coming through my front door, then do my best to kick it back out.

I need to take better care of myself, I need to get more rest.

I always admonish myself for not doing better at all of the things I know I should do—for not treating myself as I would someone I actually care for. I often find a way to make everything my fault.

You cannot leave your son the way your mother left you. Another recurring thought that leaves a pain in my gut and chest.

❧

Women who lose their mothers at young ages are petri-
fied by the idea of their own mortality when regarding
their children's lives. My mama died when I was fourteen.
With her went my anchor, my sense of safety in the world,
and my home. I cringe when I think of my son feeling the
way I did then, the way I still do, even now. I want him
to know he will always belong to someone, to someone
who will always be there. How I long for control over that
part more than I long for control over any part of this and
it's the kind that's absolutely unattainable. Damn it. I can't
leave him. I have to do everything I can think of to ensure
my own safety here now because I have to make sure he's
okay, that he has what he needs, that no one harms him.
I have lists of things to make sure of for him! The knowledge that I will leave him too early, just like my mama
left me, bangs around in my brain like a hateful ghost.
Though I try so hard not to, I will fail him. Chances are I
won't outlive him. The possibility that I could is another,
even more unwelcome vision.

❧

I looked at my watch and shook it all off as best I could.
It was four thirty in the afternoon. I didn't stop to do a
quick Google search for breast lesions on the smarty box. I
just scooped my keys from the entryway table and walked
out the door to pick up my boy from school. The short
walk there brought forth the ever-evolving checklist that

periodically goes through my head. Health insurance? Yes. I'm so glad I didn't let it lapse, though it's about to put me in the poorhouse. I'm a self-employed artist and that sort of job doesn't come with the benefits straight ones do.

I should get a job with benefits, a straight job, I thought.

Though if I have cancer, no one will hire me to do anything. I'm not exactly super-employable as it is, since I've spent my life racking up experience that's hard to put down on paper and make look like I'm qualified for anything but packing a suitcase, traveling, and making things. Back to the checklist: Life insurance? Yes. I put that in place over two years ago. He'll have enough money to be looked after when I'm gone, as long as that's within the thirty years since I got the policy. It's term, not whole life.

Should I get another whole life policy?

God, they're expensive. I'll probably die before the thirty years is done. But what if I don't? What can I give up to afford another one? I'm not rolling in cash. What about his special needs trust? Fuck. Fuck fuck fuck fuck fuck fuck fuck. I told myself I still had time to push that thought away and deal with it next year.

I picked him up from school, we walked home, and went about our usual routine. Put away backpack, take off shoes and socks, go to the bathroom, have a snack, ask him about his day, have dinner, bath time, snuggle time, watch-something-on-the-iPad time. I hugged him before he got under the covers at 8:15 that night as usual. I didn't whisper anything about my news in his ear. Living with a person who doesn't talk can be incredibly lonely, but I get by on the knowledge that he is likely enlightened about most things already, without me saying a word. He knows me as I know him, doesn't he? Does he worry that his mama will die like I worried about it when I was his age?

It was quiet in the apartment. I puttered around and considered going to bed myself, but I chewed my lip and paced about a little before I could get settled down.

It's just a thing. I told myself that over and over as I quieted the house for bedtime. Another thing that will come and then go, whatever it turns out to be. It happens every day. No big deal.

The next morning, the news of the lesion and cluster of cysts felt farther away but still present, like a looming court date, tax day, or a dinner that's more of an obligation than not. When my mind rested, there it was. The breast. Regardless, I carried on with all of the things and the days came and went as they always do. I did the two-week tour with Sissy that was on the calendar. There was work to be done and income to be earned to keep the health and life insurance premiums paid. There was a new record to promote. Nothing stopped because of the looming issue nor should it have. What was I going to do anyway? Nothing was really wrong, not yet. Most everyone goes through this at some juncture, and even though breast cancer seems to run rampant these days, I kept telling myself that this wouldn't be my year, despite what my instincts had whispered to me.

Maybe they were telling me it will happen, but later, I thought.

"I have to be positive. Women leave their children too early all the time. Worrying won't help and will likely make it worse," I said to myself when I was alone.

I worried, I didn't worry. I told myself I wasn't fine, that I surely had cancer this time, and then that I *was* fine, and that I couldn't possibly have cancer, not now, not with everything else. Surely God wouldn't be so cruel. Hadn't I had enough for the moment? But surely God isn't quite in control of such things, such things that are so very small in the big scheme. Awful thing upon awful thing piles up on people all the time. One of the mysteries of life as I see it is that there is no obvious balance in fortunes from one person to the next. Our sense of justice, however small, tricks us into thinking there must be some sort of equilibrium working somewhere, but no. There isn't a calamity limit or bad luck quota. It may be because I know this that I pray.

The few people I told mostly brushed it off as routine. The world hardly shifts or slants for anyone except the one with the lesion, lump, cluster of cysts, or whatever kind of intruder has barged in to steal their shaky peace of mind. Everybody's got their something, and their something is the most important something most of the time. Of that, I am admittedly the queen. Note to self: take head out of ass.

Even though I asked for a little mercy in my prayers, my somethings didn't let up when I got the directions to have a targeted ultrasound. Nor did they when the day for that appointment finally came and the doctor revealed to me that I had a lump 1.5 centimeters in size, which is somewhere between a pea and a peanut, and it would need to be biopsied. Another procedure, another thing. It was scheduled for three weeks later. I self-pityingly kept wondering why. Even though I know it doesn't exist, I too suppose I think there should be some give-and-take in the cosmos—you get this bad news, then you get a break somewhere else. But my bank account didn't miraculously become more padded, no one started cooking for us and making sure we had an adequate supply of toilet paper and coffee, and the honking horns and hot asphalt of the city didn't start to exhaust me any less. I tried to remember grace. I am a fortunate woman. I accepted as best I could the idea that I'd likely be having regular biopsies for the rest of my life—I have to consider dense breast tissue, family history, stressful existence, not enough rest, the 30 percent chance I already knew about—but what I couldn't think about without losing my breath was the idea that I might be sick and wouldn't be able to take care of my child.

I have no family close by. I have no family within a thousand miles of here and no parents anywhere south of heaven. Could they help with this? I honestly have thoughts like that. I ask the air for their help, calling out to them in an audible voice when I am alone as if they're hovering in the air along with the dust particles.

"Mama? Daddy? Could you step in here maybe?"

The praying is more meditation that anything, but maybe it moves some energy in a positive direction. It can't hurt, right? Maybe they can hear me even if God can't. Maybe they'll say yes even if he says no. That sounds absurd. But aren't we absurd? The tricks we play on ourselves. If we accepted the truth, that life is unbelievably painful, that most of us die horrible deaths and do it alone, wouldn't we all just go ahead and get it over with? That's a bleak thought that I don't enjoy, so yes, I pray. Maybe it helps me see the beauty in it all too, the beauty among the absurdity of going along thinking we have any power at all over anything, much less how long we get to stay on the planet. But I stick to it. It's all I've got.

"Please, don't let me be sick. Not now."

The weight of abbreviated and inadequate parenting twists around me like a heavy chain and tells me that I will fail him. It rattles and clanks as I drag it around and it distracts me. I can't shake it off. It's grown into my skin. Maybe that heavy legacy, coupled with the confusion and panic that comes with autism, makes me a better parent than I would be otherwise. Maybe they propel me into hypervigilance. But is that hypervigilance doing anyone any good? Is it good for my son that I am obsessed with his development and apparently think I should solely bear its responsibility? Is it good for me to put such pressure on myself? Is it good for us? Does hypervigilance plus dense breast tissue cause cancer? Is my hypervigilance keeping him from being as independent as he can be?

"I should give myself a break. I should let some things go sometimes," I tell myself.

I talk a good game to myself but I don't really listen. I think about trying to convince myself that so much of how he does and will do depends on him and not Every.

Little. Thing. I. Do. And. Every. Step. I. Make. The guilt over the combined MMR shot. The geriatric pregnancy. The loss he inherited.

I wonder—what if we both took a deep breath, exhaled, and found a pasture to run in for a while? What if we sat together and watched the waves from a shore somewhere for a year instead of undertaking one more full of the discrete trials of ABA therapy done behind a desk, one more full of daily notes from his school about how many times he made non-contextual hand movements and how many times he yelled, one more full of days stuck inside these claustrophobic walls and buildings, one more full of emails from this organization or that about the next autism fundraiser or latest nostrum? What if we were just allowed to be, to find our breath, for a while? There are days when I wish we could run away.

༄

The morning of the biopsy, I showered but remembered not to apply deodorant or body lotion. I dressed in loose clothing and walked John Henry to school. I then returned to our apartment to walk our eleven-year-old Chihuahua, Petey, then H. and I headed southeast to the radiologist's office. He held my hand for the entire walk and kept giving me his most reassuring smile. I acted like I didn't know what he was doing as he tried to silently convince me he wasn't worried too. We arrived; I filled out the paperwork and they called me back to the maze of exam rooms to the right of the waiting area. I put on the gown, open in the front. I knew the drill. I sat down in a chair, freezing from the air conditioning blowing directly on me, and waited for my name to be called again.

"Ms. Moyer?"

"Moorer."

"Come on back."

⌐〜

A technician waited for me in the darkened exam room with the big ultrasound machine by the table I was to lie on. I got on it after I pulled the iPod and headphones from my bag and asked if I could listen to music during the procedure. I have the urge to run like a scalded dog when I hear medical instruments clinking together—the sound of metal mixed with plastic wrappers being peeled off of pointy things nauseates me. She told me she thought it would be okay but I'd have to ask the doctor. I lay back on the table and scrolled through my albums.

The doctor came in and explained the procedure to me. I'd have to have my right arm over my head and I'd have to lie very still as she inserted first the needle with the numbing agent and then the implement that would take tiny bits of tissue from the potentially poisonous pustule inside me. I told her that would be fine, I could do that, but could I please have my music? She demonstrated with the implement the noise that it would make—it sounded like a plastic staple gun—so I wouldn't be surprised and my overactive startle reflex wouldn't make me flinch. I thanked her for the kind warning. She told me I could have my music unless it kept me from hearing her when she spoke to me. I showed her my one-ear-partially-off trick that I do when I sing in the studio. We agreed that our system would work. I started *Astral Weeks* and she started pushing on my breast after she touched my arm and assured me everything would be okay.

I was told I would feel pressure and I did. I started to cry, not out of pain but some sort of relief that I could at least then move on to the next step. This sucked, but it would be okay, as she said. I found, aided by the tempo softly pulsing in my headphones, the breath. I started to let go a little. I thought of that pasture and that shore and didn't feel the long needle-ish tool that was to clip the bits of possibly malignant tissue from my body go into me.

She took several samples, the plastic-staple-gun sound going off every ten seconds or so, but by the time I heard the intro to "Madame George," the procedure was complete. The breast was bandaged and taped. I texted H. that I was okay, but had to have a quick mammogram. I was incredulous that they'd insist on doing yet one more thing to me, but they flattened the breast like a pancake to take one last image. Finally, I walked out of the exam room. I was somehow energized, exactly like you are when something you've been dreading is over. I took off the open-in-the-front gown and got dressed. I texted my sister and the girlfriends I'd told I had to do all this mess and let them know I was okay and was headed home. H. met me in the waiting room, took my hand, walked me out to the street, hailed a cab, took me home, and made me get in bed. It was all finished. That part at least.

⤳

Three days later, John Henry, H., and I flew to the West Coast for a few tour dates. The eczema on my right hand had spread from one patch in the space between the thumb and forefinger to the fingertips of both hands, which were pulling away from my fingernails and were cracked open, bleeding, and painful, making my hands nearly useless. I moisturized and salved to no avail. Eczema is made much worse by stress. The breast was sore and itchy, but I could neither ease the ache nor scratch it. The flight was long—I'd booked a late evening thinking that my son might sleep through most of it if we got lucky, but he didn't. He took only one fifteen-minute nap during the entire six-hour flight. I was armed with movies on his iPad and his favorite snacks and emergency Skittles, but for the last hour of the flight he shouted repeatedly, probably out of utter delirium. Who could blame him? I wanted to scream my head off too. We made it from JFK to LAX, albeit in a tattered and worn state. H. and I had gotten in a terrible, stress-induced argument even before the plane left the runway.

"I am so fucking sick of you."

I knew I deserved it but it still surprised me when he said it. The truth was he wasn't alone. I was sick of me too. And I'd apparently completely eroded the patience of the dear, sweet man who'd nursed me through the pointy-needle episode two days earlier, the kind person who not only loves me but my son as well and had tried his best to make sure we were all okay before we got on the plane. We'd eaten supper in a seafood restaurant before boarding our flight and I'd warned him against leaving his credit card lying on the table for the server to come pick up at her leisure. I said that anyone could just come along and take it and then run off with it, and no matter if he canceled it right away, it would cause easily avoided up-heaval in his (my) life. My hypervigilance. He looked at me like I was crazy, explaining that an airport would be the most ridiculous place for someone to attempt such a thing since there are cameras and security guards every-where. I explained that I'd had credit card numbers stolen even when a card was in my wallet.

That's the difference between us. He's always okay and wonders what good is around the corner, almost as if he can't imagine the impending doom I know is waiting. I'm almost never okay and live as if the sky is always about to fall. His parents are still together, still alive. Maybe that's not all there is to it but I do the math and it equals a safety net of a kind I know nothing about. Then my mind returns to how my son would do without me. Then it returns to the breast, now bandaged and itchy. I know that I teeter on the edge of a hypervigilant breakdown, one that I put myself in all alone while trying to and mostly failing to ap-pear as if I have it all together. I always argue that the sky will indeed fall, that the credit card will indeed be swiped by some criminal hand. I boggle his mind with my what-if scenarios, my over-preparation, my worry. A person on high alert can be difficult to live with and I know it. If I die too soon, will my son become like me? Another absurdity of life: that we think peak awareness and well-organized to-do lists will keep us out of trouble. I've made myself physically ill to the point that my adrenal glands have all but blown out. My response system is just about ruined. Then I remind myself that I'm fine. That anything I'm going through is only life. I'm just a person, I'm just a mother, I'm just trying to get from one thing to the next just like everyone else. I'm not a failure. I won't fail my son.

Sick of myself. Indeed. I am much sicker of myself than anyone else could possibly be, but I didn't say that to H. I didn't figure there was any need and it probably wouldn't have helped him understand since he has his own list of somethings over which to have anxiety attacks. But I was sick of everything, really. I was sick of worrying about being sick. I was sick of worrying about my son being sick. I was sick of no one really even understanding autism, sick of hearing about healing the gut, sick of looking at the spines of ultimately useless books offering this cure or that, sick of there not being any kind of cure at all, sick of knowing that my life is at least half over and that my son might be alone when I die, sick of worrying about money, sick of knowing he needs to run and play more than he gets to, sick of worrying about my relationship suffering because I'm not paying enough attention to it, sick of my ridiculous neuroses, sick of no one seeing me drowning in it all, sick of my hands bleeding, hurting, and shaking all the time, sick of crying, sick of everything seeming like a mess despite my attempts to keep it all under control, sick of not being able to reach that pasture and that shore, sick of everything being so hard, sick of being exhausted, sick of not being able to locate the grace I need to get through it all with a smile on my face and without doling out warnings about credit card theft. I was also sick of being sick of it all. I was sick of not being able to find the breath.

Even once nestled at my sister's house in California that night, I felt afraid and worried, the thought of biopsy results floating through my head on average every fifteen minutes or so. A startlingly huge bruise had spread across the breast. I stared at it in the bathroom mirror after I got John Henry to sleep, and to my surprise, the breast had become something I knew less well than before, less mine somehow. It looked distorted and hurt. What was unstable but integrated had become parasitically dependent, dangerous, and at least partly foreign. I'd somehow depersonalized it and emotionally detached from it without much effort at all, and I thought I might not mind so much if it were gone. The doctor's depersonalization technique seemed to have worked.

I'd come down with a cold to top it all off. But what to do but keep going? Sissy and I played two shows together the following week and I had to keep a tissue for my runny nose in my pocket during both. She kept reminding me that it would all be okay when she sensed my mind had wandered. We wrote a song and recorded it with our band. John Henry didn't starve or get hurt due to my negligence or due to anything at all. H. didn't leave me despite his worn-thin patience. I somehow kept the plates spinning, and on the following Thursday saw "Spring OB/GYN" appear on my phone once again. I drew in the air that hung in between my lips and the screen that gave me a choice to answer, decline, or send the call to voicemail.

"We got your biopsy results and everything came back normal. You'll need to go back in six months, of course, but for now everything is okay."

The sky was still above my head and not scattered around my ankles. But it wasn't because I had willed it to be. It wasn't because I had worried so much. It wasn't because of my hypervigilance, it wasn't because I gave John Henry organic strawberries for breakfast that morning, or that I paid my bills on time, or that I'd mastered the American Sign Language alphabet and finger-spelled E-I-E-I-O every time I heard him hum "Old MacDonald," or even because he has autism and I'm an orphan and it had been decided that nothing else bad could happen to us. It just wasn't my turn. Not yet. People pray all day every day and still die in explosions or from AIDS or random gunfire. There is no law of opposites. Just because someone stacks up a list of hardships doesn't mean they ever reach a limit. And just because things seem to go okay for a while doesn't mean they won't continue to. There is no finite amount of cancer or autism or tragic death or everything being just fine to go around. I think this is why we have faith, because we *have* to have it in the face of such uncertainty. This is why I sometimes call on my mama and daddy out loud, because there is absolutely nothing else to do. Maybe my prayers and pleas worked, or maybe they didn't, but I wondered what that phone call would've revealed had I not asked for what I needed.

I'd left John Henry with a sitter and was riding in the back seat of a car with H., en route to pick up Sissy for a recording session, when the call came. He and I both smiled wide smiles and laughed, putting our foreheads together after I relayed the good news. I held my eyes closed and another silent prayer, one of gratitude, and my son's bright smile came into my mind. I was going to be okay, at least for another six months.

I get to make sure he's all right for another six months, I thought. I exhaled.

The breath. There it was.

H. squeezed my hand. When Sissy got in the car, I told her the news. Though she had claimed not to be worried, I saw relief pass over her face. We got to the studio. The band was set up and waiting for us. We entered the vocal booth and charged right into Elmore James's "Strange Angels."

Functional Behavior Assessment

He's not sleeping well. And when he does sleep, it isn't in his bed for at least a portion of the night—lately he wants to sleep with me. Sometimes I'm too exhausted to fight it and just let him stay. Sometimes I'm grateful for the quiet and stillness, his peacefulness, so I let it go. I'm not supposed to allow him to just get his way, am I? Today, it's hard to care.

I do care. *And*, as I'm supposed to, I look for reasons for the behaviors in the behaviors themselves. This is the functional behavior assessment, the FBA, if you will:

- Why is he not sleeping? Hormones, anxiety, his mind is in a loop about something, his body is uncomfortable somehow, he hears all the noises louder than I do, maybe there's a light outside his window keeping him awake, maybe he wants to know what I'm doing.

- Why is he screaming or making the same noise over and over? To hear his own voice and to stimulate himself. To try to express something that he can't say. To make himself feel like everything is okay.

- Why is he pulling my hair? To express his anger or frustration, or to try to get his way. He knows it's an effective method because I react and sometimes even give in. Sometimes I think he might do it just to do it and doesn't really have a reason—there are some pulls that seem half-hearted.

- Why is he throwing things? He likes the crashing sound. Maybe he lost control of his gross motor skills. Maybe he meant to play but didn't know how. I pick up whatever he throws or direct him to do it step-by-step if I have the time. If I have the will.

- Why is he digging his fingernails into my hand while I'm trying to hold his? He doesn't want to go where I'm taking him, something is bothering him and making him tense, he likes the sensation or resulting reaction from me. Maybe he can't help it.

- Why is he biting the back of his hand? He remembers he shouldn't bite mine or anyone else's. Or mine or anyone else's anything. Maybe he likes how it feels.

- Why does he want to sleep with me? Maybe my bed is more comfortable to him. Maybe he wants to be close to me. Maybe he's just pushing his limits.

Of course, all of those things, those assessments, could be only what I find on the surface. There could be deeper underlying causes for it all as well, to which I have no access. I wonder if I'm missing the smaller cues. I look for answers so hard sometimes that I feel like someone who observes her child rather than someone who is experiencing life with her child. I suppose some dissociation is required when parenting—we must conduct research and extend love and care at the same time. We conduct the research *because* of the love. But it's sometimes heartbreaking to watch, especially the aggression. Behaviors that don't directly involve someone else are one thing, but the ones that do are another. What distress must he be in to lash out when he is generally such a sweet, loving boy with such a, most of the time, gentle way? I'm not supposed to tell you about this part, am I? What I'm supposed to tell you is that everything is fine.

It isn't.

What it is, is finally Monday morning. John Henry is at school after what felt like one of the longest weekends of my life. It probably wasn't his idea of a great one either. I had promised to sing at the wedding of one of my best friends and was determined to show up no matter what I had to do to pull off such a thing, so we traveled from New York City to Houston and took two nearly four-hour flights to get there and back within three days. The first one, when we headed west, was stressful, worrisome, tearful. Something was bothering him. There was hair pulling, fingernail gouging, shouting, throwing whatever he could get his hands on—nothing I tried could calm him for long. We arrived in Texas in one piece but just barely. The flight back east went better, with only one hair pull, but was preceded by a terrifying drive to the airport. I'd rented a car and made the mistake of putting John Henry in the passenger seat for its return, thinking he'd like riding up front with me. He grabbed my hair and pulled my head toward him while I was navigating the interstate. We miraculously made it back to Houston Hobby without having an accident—I would've stopped and put him in the back seat if there'd been a place to pull over but there wasn't—and I made a tearful call to H. from the family-assist restroom across from our departure gate. John Henry played in the water I'd turned on in the probably disgustingly germy sink while I paced the approximately six-foot-square area. The bathroom was the only safe place I could find, the only place I could let go of his hand and give him, and myself, some space. H. convinced me that I could do it again, that we would get through it, that it wouldn't be as bad as the flight two days before had been, and that I was capable of getting through whatever scenario might transpire, that he'd seen me do it all before.

Sometimes I spiral downward into a trembling, scared mess. I take my deep breaths, I do the FBA: "What is the consequence that this or that behavior creates that causes the behavior to persist?" I whisper the mantras, which do help some, but not always. It's hard to be peaceful and rational inside what feels like a crisis. Is it really a crisis? No, not in the big scheme. But my scalp is still sore.

I don't even want to touch my head. I've just sat down at my desk to write and the only words that will come are these. These are not the ones that I wish were in my mind. I study the gouges covering the backs of my hands and sides of my thumbs. They look awful. I feel ashamed. I try to sort out my emotions by doing what I always do. I go back to the beginning. I do an FBA on myself.

❦

My beginning was in an abusive, violent, and unpredictable household. Life, now, also sometimes feels like that, if in a completely different way. Yes, I know this is my child and this is not at all, not even remotely, the same situation, but only my mind knows the difference—my body doesn't know it until I tell it. I'm talking about what happens when past trauma meets a situation that feels out of control and dangerous. It isn't hard to figure out what happens to me, even though I'm here and not there anymore. None of that is my son's fault, but my knowledge of that doesn't take the feeling away.

- Why do I panic when I feel assaulted or threatened? I don't feel safe. I'm afraid I'm going to die or something else undoable and tragic will happen.
- Why do I feel ashamed, guilty, and why do I sometimes take it personally? No one ever told me it isn't all my fault.
- Why do I sometimes get angry? I am human.

My issues and triggers aren't and shouldn't be the focus. I should do better. I should rise above it all somehow and take care of my boy and whatever else needs taking care of without consideration of anything but him. Isn't that what a good mother does? I'm supposed to be made of 100 percent love and devotion and 0 percent concern for my own well-being, aren't I? I'm not. I'm not supposed to tell you that either. Wait—the oxygen mask theory everyone is always talking about—take care of yourself first so you can then take care of someone else. What if I can't reach the damn thing because I'm using my hands to try to get his fingers loosened from my hair?

My mind and body wrestle. My mind tells me that I am not really being threatened, that I can handle this, that he doesn't mean to hurt me and the only reason he does is because I'm not meeting his needs. I know I can figure out what they are if I try hard enough, can't I? If I can just do that, I can fix this. My body tells me something different. It tells me that there is a threat, that I am not safe here. I fight my way past that thought and remind myself that everything I've worked so hard to learn about respecting myself, about loving myself, about maintaining proper boundaries, about not allowing anyone to mistreat me doesn't apply here.

None of the rules apply here at all.

This requires an entirely new set—one that might need to be rewritten at any moment because the game changes constantly. I worry that I can't keep up. I remind myself that this is parenting, that this is love. Indeed, it is both. What I also know is that this is complicated and hard to figure out some days. I go from one thought to another. Am I the perfect candidate to deal with this sort of challenge? Why not me, right? I can handle anything. Am I the worst possible candidate for this because I'm emotionally worn down and fraught even outside of this? Why me? I obviously can't handle anything at all. Why me? Why not me? Why not me? Why me? Doesn't matter. We're in it. We're doing this. Doesn't matter if I'm doing it wrong. Can I detach and stay attached? Can I not take this personally and stay personally involved? Can I be both his mama and his caretaker?

I know. I know. Why would I do such a thing as fly halfway across the country with him if it is so hard? It's a popular question. Some of the flights we take are nearly flawless. John Henry is capable of calmer behavior than most typical children his age. And stopping life for autism or almost any other reason is a choice I can't bring myself to make. Friends' weddings are important. Living life despite difficulty is important. Not only for me, but for him. When we have a tough flight, I usually don't know why, so it's not as if I can just do all the right things to ensure it all goes smoothly. It isn't as if I forget some important element to make sure we're successful. I do try, but there is no way for me to catch everything. I don't know what's going on with him at all times. I'm not always able to understand, FBA or not.

Recommendations for dealing with an aggressive autistic child, gathered from years of reading and talking to teachers and other parents:

Find the cause for the aggression.

Sometimes I can, sometimes I can't.

It could be some sort of distress or pain that isn't visible.

Yes, I know. God, however do I know and however does it haunt me. Where is my checklist?

It may be an interruption to their routine.

We adhere to our routine, which sometimes means there is no routine. Besides, I know that he has pulled my hair because he wants my iPad and I won't give it to him so that gives me evidence that he sometimes uses this tactic to get something he wants and on that behavior I have to turn my back because that's just brattiness, of which everyone is capable.

It may be anger, fear, insecurity, anxiety.

I know, I know, I know, I know. I rub his back, I hold his hand, I tell him it's all right no matter what. I wait for the reassuring hug and the pat on the back that he'll ultimately give me when it has passed. I offer anything at my disposal to try to make it better. Sometimes nothing works and I can only helplessly wait for it to end.

It may be an attempt to gain attention.

Yes, it may be. How can I come up with more attention to give? If I'm sitting right beside him on an airplane with a bag of gummy bears in my hand to dole out in exchange for good behavior, am I not attending sufficiently? We sit in the bulkhead of the plane if we can so there's nothing going on in front of us. I can't control the sounds, the smells, or the amount of people on the plane.

After the cause is identified, remove it.

I cannot remove the world.

I cannot predict his every need before it arises, and even when it does.

We cannot parachute out of the airplane, though I've fantasized about just such a thing.

Should I shave my head?

Is he testing me? He could be angry with me about something that I did or didn't do. He may be emotionally hurt or someone might have mistreated him somehow and I didn't see it. My guilt takes over—if only I could do this better. If only I were better at shielding him from the onslaught just being here brings. If only I didn't insist on living my life and kept him off of four-hour flights.

I again work the FBA. I know he has no deep, hidden agendas. Though the causes for my behavior and responses to the world and even this may be rooted in dark emotional corners, his may not be. There is only survival for him in these moments. And how I respond is, sadly, probably always triage—I can only bandage, not heal. Everything I do to assuage whatever effect is being displayed does nothing to rid him of the cause, the cause that is hidden from me. I want nothing more than to take whatever it is away.

⁓

Effect. Effects. Am I allowed to think of those? When someone, anyone, hurts us in whatever way, we are told to get away from that person and into a safe environment. I cannot and do not want to get away from my child. I only want to make whatever is wrong okay. I don't want to do any of the things I would typically want to do.

This isn't typical. This is autism.

That this is autism doesn't stop me from being triggered. How do we come out of these moments unscathed and with our relationship intact? I worry about the cumulative effects. There have been periods of time when I braced myself against him, when outbursts were just as likely as hugs. I don't want a trauma bond with my son. How do I protect us both?

Sometimes I want to shout. Sometimes I want to say things I shouldn't say.

Sometimes I want to scream. Sometimes I want to whisper, "You don't even like me." I don't. I know it isn't true.

We often say that people with autism don't or can't understand the neurotypical world. We don't understand people with autism either. We don't receive their messages the way they're intended because we aren't hearing them the right way. We don't know the right way to listen. I don't have the key to crack that code, even now, this far down the line, and I might not ever discover it. I keep looking. I don't need to do a functional behavioral assessment to figure out why.

Promises

March 2020. The first month of the coronavirus pandemic. We'd moved to Nashville the summer before, so we at least got to spend more time outside than we would've had we still been living in New York, but sheltering in place was still a challenge. Everyone was thrown off and John Henry was no exception.

He had spent the previous six months in his usual school in New York, but living with his dad and without me, per an agreement we'd reached the previous year. John Henry wasn't due to come back home until the beginning of summer, so we all had to adjust, and quickly, when he arrived. After the previous summer's home therapy program, when most of his work was done outside and in person, I'm sure he wondered why he was having to do sessions with his New York teachers over the computer, but we had to do whatever we could to keep things, and him, on course.

⌒

I set up a work area in his bedroom. I Velcroed a token board to the wall above where I'd positioned a table and two chairs. I made a pile of the best reinforcers I could come up with—a bin of slime, a bin of water, another bin of water beads, spinners, Mardi Gras beads, water wigglers, musical cause-and-effect toys, candy, gum. OK Go and Adele videos were at the ready on the iPad—anything I could think of that he loves. I organized a self-care bag identical to the one he uses at school for bathroom breaks. Each evening, I taped the schedule I received from his head teacher to his bedroom door in preparation for the next day. It hung alongside the master lists of exercises the occupational therapist sent and summer goals to try to reach by the time school resumed in the fall. Homeschooling took a lot of thought, preparation, and patience—it's a lot for any parent to homeschool, period, especially when it comes as a surprise—but we plowed through. I was always relieved when the day's sessions were finished, but coming up with fun things to do wasn't easy either. I'd talk to John Henry about why we couldn't go anywhere—not to the park, not to the swimming pool at the Y or to any of the pools at our friends' houses, not to the ice-cream shop down the street. We took car rides to friends' houses for driveway visits and sometimes to nowhere at all. We went for walks in the eerily quiet neighborhood. We made trips to get milkshakes for progressions and successes. We got a new bicycle to practice riding. We celebrated John Henry's tenth birthday as best we could—with cake, balloons, and that new bicycle, but unfortunately not much else. There was a routine of sorts, but not one like we'd ever had before.

My favorite time during that period was spent in the backyard. It's our happiest place. I had gotten the raised-bed garden planted and spent as much time as I could babying it. We had tomatoes, lettuces, cucumbers, peppers, herbs, my beloved potted boxwoods and cypress trees, a few pretty rose bushes, and as many flowers as I could plant all growing around us. John Henry would happily play on his splash pad or his giant lagoon—a double-bed-sized, transparent, thick vinyl pod you fill with water—as I'd tend to our plants and vegetables and try to teach him to water them when his desire for control of the hose got too strong for him to resist, thinking that in a few years I could hand the job over to him. We'd gotten a new rescue puppy—a black Lab mixed with something else even bigger—who, along with our Jackhuahua, Willie (we lost Petey in September 2018), loved to fuss around back there with us. H. would often be in the studio, a small, one-room building just steps away from our back door, recording music. We were figuring out how to do livestream shows from home to keep some income coming in. We'd finished a tour a month earlier during which we put ourselves, unknowingly at the beginning of it, at high risk, but neither one of us had gotten the virus by mid-April.

We took that as a good sign. John Henry and his father had come down from New York right after the schools closed and neither one of them had any symptoms either. We were not sick. It felt like we would be okay. We stayed at home like we were told to do, and though we were bustling with activity, life had a slower, more basic feeling. It felt lucky, our situation. I felt forever home, when the lack of work, the shutdown of the economy, and the possible increase in scarcity of services for my son didn't creep into my mind. I could picture us right there—digging in our dirt, growing vegetables and flowers and trees, and making music and writing and learning and being a family—forever. I didn't know how we'd fare emotionally, intellectually, or economically, but we were so much more fortunate than most who were facing the same things. I was grateful.

I worried over John Henry even more than usual if that's possible and tried to pick up any clue I could about how he was doing emotionally. I was always stocked up on his favorite snacks, introduced him to new ones, bought him new movies to watch that I either noticed he showed an interest in or just thought he might like—anything to bolster the sense of safety and love I always hope surrounds him. I had no idea how it all was affecting him. I tried to make his therapies as much fun as I could, though I feared regression so much I'm sure he could feel the anxiety seeping out of my pores. He had made significant progress in self-care the several months before, but upon arrival in Tennessee, he went a bit backward.

We struggled more over brushing teeth and hair, using the bathroom appropriately and consistently, dressing, and following directions than we had in a while. We spent a few months turning the unwanted trajectory around, and as it usually goes, it was two steps forward, one step back for what seemed like too long, but I knew the cause, or at least most of it—the sudden change in structure, environment, and routine. Though John Henry is increasingly able to adapt to changes, he still thrives on structure as most of us do. And who knows what he knew? How does one explain a pandemic to a child at all, much less one who can't ask questions? I wondered what I should say. I've often worried about how he receives that sort of information—the kind about something bad or concerning happening—what does it mean to him? Is it overwhelming for him to think about? How does he contextualize the things I tell him? I have said that I think he knows everything. More importantly, I think he *feels* everything.

A Wednesday, after supper. My boy loves to soak in the bathtub, so after we washed his hair and all the important parts, I left him to lie in the water for a while and returned to the kitchen. I cleaned up from the cooking I'd done and worked on getting everything ready for the next day, then went back to the bathroom to check on him. He was still lying on his back, with only his face sticking out of the water. He stared up at the ceiling. I crouched down by the tub to try to get eye level with him.

"Hey, babe. How you doing in here?"

His eyes shifted to mine.

"Hey," I quietly said again.

He slowly moved his right arm out of the water and extended it toward me. I almost braced myself but didn't. Then I felt his hand cup the left side of my face. His eyes were locked with mine. He was smiling, slightly, and giving me his most lovely eyes—peaceful, deep, and kind. The tenderness immediately created tears in mine. I'm used to receiving routine hugs and pats on the shoulder and back from him when I pull him close, but I'd rarely gotten anything like this. This felt like a deliberate bid for connection, like he was trying to tell me something, or trying to get me to tell *him* something, or . . . like he was seeing me. Like he was telling me it was all going to be okay somehow.

I held his gaze. Those eyes, the most mysterious blue—a blue that is sometimes the sort of dark you see only when you're looking at a very cold and very deep ocean. A blue that's sometimes the color of the sky in winter, when it is crisp. A blue that no one can quite believe when they see it. A blue that takes my breath away too, even now.

❧

The bonds of parenthood are staggering to me. Whatever sort of love it is that is created in us when we have children—and it springs out, Athena-like, fully formed from the first smell of them—is the sort that also gives us, if not short memories, then an ability to put our injuries, disappointments, and hurts away at the slightest appearance of kindness from them. One ounce of warmth from my son takes away a hundred pounds of what can sometimes feel like indifference. How does that happen if not by divine creation? What we know and intrinsically feel is actually a miracle, isn't it? As what was happening between us as I crouched beside the bathtub.

I didn't stop to do an FBA. Isn't it funny that I think a behavior I don't like could be rooted in a million different causes, but this one, that I did like, could only mean something positive: that my son was reaching out to me out of affection for me. That he wanted to let me know something. That he was able to connect to his feelings and then express them to me. This had to mean approval, happiness, success, love, didn't it? Call it confirmation bias. The truth is, he could've just been fascinated by my eyes. He could've just wanted to feel the texture of my skin. He could've wanted to feel my jaws move as they made words. I have no way of knowing the truth about why he reached his hand out to touch my face. I only know what I chose to believe and how good it felt to believe it.

He held my face in his hand for at least a minute. Then he slid his arm back down into the water. I stayed put, never averting my eyes from his. Then he did it again.

I was amazed, but I worried that his touch might turn harsh when he patted my cheek just a little that time. I'd experienced that before. I turned my face away just slightly and he stopped the patting. He understood my boundary and just held his hand there, again, and fixed his gaze on me. I held mine on him. We drifted off together—floating on a cloud of curiosity and familiarity, of unknowing and knowing, of faith and grace. I would've stayed there until the water turned cold.

He slid his arm back beneath the surface of the water again and shifted his eyes back toward the ceiling. He was so beautifully calm lying there in the water that I didn't move for another minute or so. My mind spun with questions about what had just happened between us, yet the peacefulness that he seemed to embody fell over me as well. I waited a few beats, then I left the bathroom, heart swollen.

⌇

I thought about it all the time during the days after. The days that felt like one nameless day that never ended, when consciousness, or maybe it was some sort of semi-consciousness because we couldn't bear to pay full attention to what was happening in the world, only shifted with often-troubled sleep. I'm still thinking about it now, and it's been a few weeks since it happened and the day is still never-ending. I thought about what had brought it on. I thought about what it meant. I thought about him. I am always thinking about him. Maybe I do now more than ever, during this time of forced, endless togetherness, during this time of no school outside the house, during this time of no therapists except through the laptop, during this time of no babysitters. It's just us. Maybe *that's* it? Could it be that the new circumstances make him happy? Maybe he likes that life has slowed down and we aren't constantly traveling and juggling schedules. Maybe he likes seeing me on the other side of the worktable instead of a revolving cast of professionals. I remember how I longed for my mama some school days, how I would reluctantly get out of the car when she'd drop me off at Chatom Elementary, and how a few times I refused to get out of the car at all because of the anxiety I felt about her leaving me there. And I liked school. It wasn't that I didn't want to go, it was that I didn't want her to leave my sight. That he might feel that way makes it all rise up in me again, but it has sharper edges now, whetted by my general lack of knowledge about how he feels.

I certainly like having him home, but I *always* like having him home. I don't relish having to execute the therapies that he needs on my own, and though we typically function in a way that resembles one big discrete trial, or at least one lifelong incidental learning session, I try to keep that all balanced with just being his mama. I figured out very early on in this journey that I want to be the person he can depend on to be a soft place, someone who guides him but doesn't make him perform all the time. Someone who holds him close but also turns him out to face the world and gives him the strength and courage to go into it. The truth is, I am more than just his mama and all of the things that title normally implies. I am both his mama and his therapist. I am both his mama and his friend. I am both his mama and his advocate. I try to fill all the spaces that need filling in his life, and there are a lot of them. I've often thought that the connectedness created due to the requirements that I fill can even act as an inflammatory agent—like any child, he tests *my* limits before he tests anyone else's. Unlike any child, he does it in sometimes atypical ways. But the flip side of that is that he gives me what sometimes feels like atypical tenderness. What typical ten-year-old boy spontaneously holds his mama's face in his hands and stares into her eyes for a prolonged amount of time?

I felt lucky to have had such an experience. I felt lucky to have such a child. It isn't as if I forgot how hard it can all be because he was so sweet that evening in the bathtub—he got out of it that night and I still had to towel him off, get him to use the toilet, and dress him in his pajamas—things that a typical ten-year-old could do for himself—but the sweetness we'd experienced made all of those things feel effortless. It put a gust of wind under my sails, which put more under his. There was more yang to balance the yin.

I wanted more of those tender moments. I wanted more of that calm, quiet sweetness. I reminded myself to be satisfied with what I'd gotten, and to look further into myself for the things that I'd taken with me from that warm and kindhearted tub-time moment—the calm, the peace, the feeling that, yes, it does get better and, yes, things might turn out all right. When I allow myself to do that, I always come up with the same answers. Maybe what I need to do is let life be a little bit, like we're being forced to do right now. I'm so afraid of not doing "everything we can," even when I know somewhere down deep that doing everything we can to the point of utter exhaustion is not the complete answer to this question. John Henry needs help, and a significant amount of it, but he also needs me to loosen up, to spend more time in the garden with the things I love while he does the same. I feel that and I know that. I have been so concerned with progress, with trying to make sure he does as many therapeutic activities that he can stand, with making sure he has the best professional help, with making sure he has the best of *everything* that I can figure out how to get him, that maybe I've been missing the point. Are all those things all that he needs? Have I stopped to think enough about what he might *tell* me he needs or am I too busy deciding for him? I know the answer is no, but I can't always figure out how to keep it all together and simultaneously offer more of an undistracted me. I try, but I fail. Even so, it is my intention to hear what he's telling me. When I listen, I can.

Ten Minutes

I need to take a shower before I take him to school. I have
a lot of things to do today, one of which is to attend a
meeting at 10 a.m., and it has to be now. It's hard—okay,
almost impossible—to take a shower sometimes when he's
here and I'm alone with him. It's better when I can keep
my eyes on him every minute, but sometimes I have no
choice but to look away unless I want to present myself to
the world in a not-so-fresh state.

Okay. What are my steps? The door that opens onto
the hallway of the building is bolted and the chain lock
is fastened. The oven is off and the burners are as well.
There are no open containers or cans. He's set with his
iPad. The door to my bedroom is closed because I've already made the bed and he delights in unmaking it. He
also loves fooling with the things I have on top of my
dresser and I'm terrified he'll discover the heart-shaped

box with the name-tag pin in it that belonged to my mama and misplace it, throw it, put it in his mouth, and not only harm himself with the pin but chew it up. Such has been the fate of more than one treasure.

I go into the bathroom. I turn on the shower. I leave the bathroom door open. I take off my clothes and step in. I stand under the shower stream and lather up with my favorite poppy-scented soap. Ah, the little pleasures of life. I swear sometimes they're what keep me sane. In about a minute he is pulling back the curtain. He tries to get in with me.

"No, baby, it's Mama's turn for a bath."

I gently push him back from the shower. Water splashed on the floor while he was holding the curtain open so I have to make sure he doesn't slip and fall while making sure I don't either. I pull the curtain closed. He pulls it open again and jumps up and down and makes his excited noise. I return it to the closed position.

"No, baby. Mama's taking a shower right now and you can't get in."

I am embarrassed that he is seeing me naked. I don't know what he thinks about it. Does it register? He opens the curtain again.

"No!"

He leaves it alone and moves on.

What is that splashing sound? Oh shit. I forgot to close the lid to the toilet. I knew I'd forget something. I open the shower curtain and see that his arm, up to his elbow, is in the toilet bowl and he's sloshing the water around. I have just lathered up my hair. I stick my face around the shower curtain.

"Honey, get your hand out of the toilet."

He ignores me. I watch him grab my incense holder from the windowsill just above the toilet and begin to use it to stir the toilet water. *Was there pee in there?* I try to rinse my hair enough so I can get out of the shower. I step, dripping wet, onto the tile floor and walk, naked, over to him. I care less about my nudity than I did a few minutes ago, but I am still embarrassed. Nonetheless—I remember that the maintenance department for our building recently had to replace the entire toilet because a bottle of perfume was thrown in and got wedged inside it, making it impossible to flush. I have to address the situation. I remove the incense holder from his hand and close the lid to the toilet.

"John Henry, please go back to the living room while I finish my shower."

He leaves. I step back into the shower. I rinse the shampoo from my hair. I locate the conditioner, pump ten times, and haphazardly slather it on my hair. I grab my razor and go after my armpits, the left one first, then the right, trying not to cut myself as I wield the pink Daisy, Schick, Bic, or whatever the hell it is like a ninja would a sword. Done. I hear John Henry in the bathroom again. He pulls back the shower curtain.

"No, baby, it's Mama's turn for a shower, not yours. Give me just a few more minutes."

I pull the curtain closed.

I hold the razor in my right hand, the bar of soap in my left, and tend to my legs. I cut my right ankle. I always do that when I'm in a hurry. I hear John Henry making noise in the bathroom again. I pull back the shower curtain and see that he has gone to his bedroom, procured the bin designated for water play from under his bed, and put it in the sink. He turns the hot water on full blast to begin filling it.

"It's not time for water play, precious."

I twist myself around and extend my arm to reach the sink and turn the water off. He then steps over to the toilet and flushes it, which makes the water in the shower turn scalding hot. I step out from under the water until it turns cooler, silently thanking God that there is room enough for me to evade the boiling-hot stream. I rinse my hair as he leaves again.

I turn off the shower. I apply some body oil and then towel off. I wrap my rat's nest of hair in a towel. I put on my robe. I remove the water-play bin from the sink and set it on the edge of the bathtub. I wipe up the wet floor with the bath mat. I wonder how the extended stress hasn't made me some version of mad. I wonder if I am mad and don't realize it? I hear his iPad going. I walk to the living room and find him watching it but for whatever reason he is naked from the waist down. I sigh and laugh a little. I am somehow exhausted before we've even left for school, but I am also somehow clean. A victory, no matter how small or how it is achieved, is a victory all the same.

The Line

I removed every piece of art from the apartment walls. I stacked as many of the smaller pieces as I could on top of the dining room table for easy wrapping, leaving two rectangular, placemat-sized pieces of space on which to have our meals for the next four days. I leaned the larger pieces against the wall to the right of the entryway.

We're leaving.

John Henry walked into the living room a little while after my flurry and looked around as if to say, "What's going on here? Why are you dismantling our house?" I think the sudden change threw him off a little. Seeing everything start to shift from "we live here" to "we almost don't live here" threw me off a little too, but my brain quickly began to adjust as I acknowledged the line I'd just crossed. A space can transition from home to mere holding place in less than an hour, and somehow the mental

133

shift shows up on the heels of the physical rearranging. You live somewhere in the morning, then by nightfall you don't anymore.

Five more nights. The movers come on Wednesday.

❧

We've lived here since just before he turned five years old. He turned nine this April. That's almost half his life. Here must be the place he knows better than anywhere else. I wonder if he will miss it? Will his stomach feel funny, the way I know mine will, the first night we're no longer living here? Does it feel funny now, the way mine does, seeing everything go from whole to pieces in what has been our nest, our safe spot? He never misses anything, not that I can tell, so of course he'll feel it. In his stomach and likely everywhere else, and if my suspicions are correct, he'll feel it even more than I will. I've always said moving takes years off a life—the wear and tear on the body and mind, the juggling of the quotidian that must be maintained while removing roots from one place and planting them in another, the attempt to make the transition seamless, the stress of it all. It's physical and emotional upheaval, even when it's positive. But it also allows, even encourages, a certain focus on what is essential and what is not as we sift through our belongings, as we sort the tangible and decide what is and isn't worthy of a place in the abstract future we hold in a slippery vision.

❧

I start clearing out John Henry's room while he watches television. I've told myself that I will be ruthless in this process. The truth is, he doesn't play with most of the toys here and I've held on to this or that one without really asking myself why. I knew there was no real need to hang on to electric cars or Lego sets. He's not really interested in those things yet beyond a glance and initial investigation. Now I *am* asking. Why did I keep most of these things? Maybe I thought he'd one day begin to play with them properly and I was just waiting. Maybe I thought they made him feel cozy and safe, like they make me feel. Maybe I'm sentimental.

～

I sit in front of the bookshelf filled with toys and do a quick appraisal. There's no need to keep the Fisher-Price record player with the pastel-colored discs. He never played with it independently even though he seemed to enjoy it when I showed it to him four or five years ago. But maybe he didn't like it at all, because for a boy with such strength, he hasn't figured out how to pinch and twist the knob in front to make the music box inside play. Pincer grasp. That's what's required. Toy designers are amazing at embedding ways for children to learn and practice their developmental skills through play. In this case, the skill is a fine motor one. John Henry has trouble with fine motor. Even after seven years of occupational therapy, he still sometimes gets angry or frustrated when he's asked to purposefully manipulate something with his hands. Anything he has to labor over feels like work, I guess, since he has to practice his skills all the time instead of just being allowed to use them when he needs to. He doesn't seem to remember to use them incidentally, and instead seems to prefer to use his hands in ways that have no apparent purpose, in ways that are called "non-contextual" in our world. They move but they don't accomplish things that are always meaningful according to the rules by which most of us go. He fingers Mardi Gras beads and small figurines, rubber bands and squiggly fidgets, he presses the buttons on easy-to-operate, music-playing, battery-run cause-and-effect machines, or, most recently, he carries around the rack from the toaster oven. I think keeping his hands busy in such ways is a coping mechanism. They help him deal with the world and he stays busy doing that. Working on pincer grasp moves down the list of important things to learn if you're trying to survive the constant bombardment of life and the universe, if it's a challenge to make it make some sort of sense.

෴

I drift away from my purpose. Maybe he will relax a little if we can hear the birds sing better. Maybe he'll slow down if there's room to move. Maybe getting away from here for a while really *will* be . . .

෴

Where was I? I put the Fisher-Price record player in a box for donation.

There's the jack-in-the-box. Bunny-in-the-box, rather. What pops out when you turn the crank is a soft bunny. He's had this since he was a baby. I might've even bought it before he was born. He still carries it around sometimes but he never uses that same required pincer grasp to turn the crank, so appropriate use of the toy has never been achieved.

"Why do we worry so much about what's appropriate?" I mutter to myself.

Since he was a baby. I think about him as a baby, I think about myself when he was a baby. Everything he did delighted me. I tried to do my part just right—all the exclusive breastfeeding, book reading, organic food buying, all the appropriate developmental-stage toys. I think about what I assumed our trajectory would be. I had a different kind of hope then. I want to make us T-shirts that say "We don't go by the developmental chart."

My mind circles like a lazy Susan. That word—*hope.* I imagine it as just a word and break it down to letters. H-O-P-E. But it isn't just a word, is it? They aren't all created equal. *Hope* is small in size, just four letters, but does any other combination hold so much within it? No definition can do it justice. It's ultimately a word that can only be defined by its own self. And that definition is everything. That definition is everything good in the world. We do nothing good if we have no hope. If we have no hope, we have no reason. If we have no hope, we don't buy things like toys for our children. If I hadn't had hope, I wouldn't be looking at record players and bunnies-in-the-box this minute. I glance around the room. Most everything here has hope attached to it. *I hope he'll like this. I hope this will hold his attention. I hope this will make him smile.*

I think a minute—can he not willfully make pincer grasp so he can turn the crank on the bunny-in-the-box? Does his brain not tell his fingers how to do it independent of outside, hand-over-hand instruction? Maybe he does get it but it isn't meaningful to him. Maybe he doesn't care enough about playing with toys to use it. I picture myself picking up a blueberry—that's it. I picture him doing the same—sometimes he uses pincer grasp to pick up one at a time and sometimes he uses his hand like a shovel to get a handful. So do I.

I put the bunny in the donation box.

༼

I sort through more—unopened boxes of cars and trains, games sent from well-meaning relatives. They've languished here, all representing some milestone or developing interest that still waits like a moving target, one day far in front of us, then closer the next, then far away again. The books—he loves his books—here's *Dress Me Elmo*. It has buttons to button and shoelaces to tie. It looks almost brand-new. I bought it before he turned two, before we crossed the line, the one that separates before and after.

We crossed that line in March 2012. After we received confirmation of John Henry's autism via evaluation from the autism clinic at Vanderbilt in Nashville, I dove in—researching ABA, Floortime, Son-Rise, Feldenkrais,

speech therapy, occupational therapy, ordering this sup-
plement, trying that diet. It was a lot to absorb, but what
else was there to do but absorb it? Life, for my son and
for me, for his father, changed so much in such a short
time. Three hours of school in the morning, five hours
of therapy in the afternoons at home with four different
therapists, back and forth in the car, here and there. All
while I tried to maintain some semblance of a career and
life of my own. Though John Henry was born in New
York City, I decamped for Nashville after I knew something was going on. When something messed-up happens
or your life tilts on its axis in such a way, you just want
to go where you feel safest. I'd moved to Nashville the
day I finished college at twenty years old and had lived
there longer than I'd ever lived anywhere. It was home. I
also needed to be there for work. As I struggled to keep
my son from disappearing into what looked then like a
cognitive nuclear winter, I struggled to keep myself from
disappearing into it too. I knew I had to show up for myself somehow, even in those early days, so I went home. I
juggled, I worked, I made an effort to keep us both connected to the general world instead of agreeing to with-
draw into the very specific one of autism.

John Henry made an effort too, but even with daily
speech therapy sessions he wasn't getting his language
back. He would sometimes have a pop-out—a word that
was in his vocabulary before the regression—but there
was no consistency. None seemed to be developing either
but it was such early days, we were certain there would be

some soon. His behaviors were changing but not going away despite the hours of redirecting and incentivizing we provided. It felt like a race against time and encroaching dark—like the longer he was neurologically tangled up, the longer it would take for it all to become untangled. We knew he needed even more intervention than he was getting, and there were schools in New York where he could get more, and more consistency, under one roof, so we came back to where he was born and where his father was. Another shift. Another line.

That was six years ago. Every one of those years now feels blurry. Though they all have the same autism-shaped center, and they all have extreme low and high points, their edges are all smeared, one into the other, like watercolors made more watery because of a spill or loss of control. Years awash in routine, embedded techniques, IEPs, masteries, progressions, regressions, mysteries, joy, sadness, contentment, anxiety, exhaustion. Our years aren't delineated by what grade John Henry is in or what summer programs he might participate in, rather by where we are in abilities and progressions. The trajectory isn't a strictly forward one. I think about that crisp week in October 2015 when he said two words in as many days. I thought language was on its way back when that happened and his father did too—I remember him saying to me on the phone when I reported the news of the words to him, "He's going to talk"—but turns out it wasn't, not in the way or on the timeline that I thought, that we thought, it might be. That emergence might've been a stepping-stone to something that's still coming, but the last word I heard him say was about two years ago when he pronounced "doggie" as clear as day upon seeing one in the elevator of our building. Nothing comprehensible since then. That's a line I'm waiting for him to cross again. Who can know if we are near it? Days are long, years are short, and with every new one comes another realization that we're still not there. *There* might be further away than it has ever been. Meanwhile, we are here and we have to do the best we can with what we've got now.

          ~

Here. Here was once there, wasn't it? Here—this place that has the best and worst of everything. This place that has the best and brightest, the specialists and the experts and the towers one must climb to reach them. This sensory overload disguised as city. Here isn't there anymore. I don't know where there is, ultimately, or even if there is a there anymore, but I do know life changes. It has to. You can either fight it or go with its flow. I think about that, about my fear of changing what we're doing even though I know we once again have to take a chance. We once again have to gather our hope, allow ourselves to open up, and cross another line—one that separates what we've got from what may be possible.

          ~

I go through the drawers of therapeutic and teaching materials—flash cards, sets of pictures for matching, bags of Velcro for attaching PECS, blocks for stacking, beads for stringing, puzzles with their pieces attached in Ziplocs, construction paper for scribbling and snipping, wooden clothespins and paper plates cut in half for practicing that same pincer grasp. Is there anything here that we should keep? I set aside a few things that might be useful and the rest goes in the donation box.

~

I feel my energy seep away and my head lower a little as I sit. My center hurts. I wonder what the nagging inside will manifest—something shitty, probably. Most of the tiny deaths that a person dies go by without much notice, at least in the moment. But unacknowledged grief leaves marks. And even though I know I'm supposed to keep my chin up and only think about how much we *do* have, there is also sorrow. I let my tears fall. I can't get around my sadness while I do this. I don't want my son to be different from how he is except in the ways that would make his life easier, but I long to know him better. I regret that he cannot tell me more about his wants, needs, and wishes. What toys would he like to keep?

I begin to go through his collection of stuffed animals. He's hardly ever seemed to notice them except on occasion. I sort them, noting that sorting is something I learned to do with ease, only saving the ones from movies—Arlo from *The Good Dinosaur*, Woody from *Toy Story*, Poppy and Branch from *Trolls*—plus one teddy bear that I find too adorable to let go. I think about what I just did and wonder why it's so hard for John Henry to do the same. Or does he just not care to do it? I then remember how he, while watching *Toy Story* on television one afternoon in the living room right around the corner from where I sit, came to this bin and picked Woody out of the pile. That's sorting. He *can* do it. He knows what he's thinking and doing even if it seems to come and go. Does it come and go? Or does he just sort when it suits him?

~~~

Here. There. How exactly does hope shift from one thing you pinned it on to the next you think might hold it? What miraculous powers four letters can have. The taking down of the artwork, the cleaning out of his room, the mental shift that shows up on the heels of the physical rearranging—every movement helps it along somehow, every faithful thought keeps it alive. It sparks and buzzes in my mind, the flicker getting stronger. When we act out of hope, it generates itself, growing and attaching to us as we take the steps it propels us toward.

It all rushes back. My childhood, music, my parents, my sister, school, relationships, college, marriage, dreams come true, deaths, heartbreak, befores and afters, leaps, dives, happiness, rainy days, avoidances, airplanes, loves. All those lines I've crossed. My life as movie trailer complete with appropriate soundtrack fills up my brain and my ears. My vision flashes with the speed of my thoughts.

Then they land. They slow down. They cross another line, the most important one I've ever crossed, the line that gives me the faith to stand at the one we're looking at now and brave it. A boy—birth, love, joy, smiles, laughs, tears, anguish, trust, faith, fatigue, belief, the bluest eyes I've ever seen. I know that I will soon add this moment to the reel. I am still. I lift my head.

Shift Change

"John . . . Henry, John Henry, John Henry, John Henry, John Henry, John Henry, John Henry. John Henry, John Henry, John Henry, John Henry, John Henry, John Henry, John Henry. John Henry, John Henry, John Henry, John Henry, John Henry, John Henry, John Henry. John Henry, John Henry, John Henry, John Henry, John Henry, John Henry, John Henry."

I started picking him up and singing that song to him before he was a year old, stretching out the first "John" and leaning over to the right to his effervescent smiling delight. The "Henry" that followed was paired with a big sway to the left. Every other word went with a switch to the other side. He loved it. He loved hearing his name and loved the dancing. I still want to do it. *He* still wants me to do it. To do so almost takes me down; his feet hanging past my knees, his weight just thirty or so pounds shy of my own.

He is still my baby. He is my boy. He will always be those things.

He is also his father's.

His father and I disagree on many things, hence our divorce. We're lucky that we're able to find common ground on most John Henry–related matters, such as education, treatments and therapies, vacations, and the like, but the business of residential location is not one of the things on which we share the same opinion. I am, at this stage of my life, not a New York City person. John Henry's father is. I wanted to leave New York City for a softer life. John Henry's father did not. I wanted John Henry to have a softer life with me. John Henry's father did not agree that he should.

We battled about it for over a year. I wanted to leave New York City and was tired of being told I couldn't unless I left my son behind. It was ugly and I wish I'd found a better way to address our differences—we couldn't have a conversation without going for each other's most vulnerable spots—accusing, attacking, condemning, belittling—we said all of the things that unsuccessfully divorced people who share a child say and more. Then I dropped it, just before we had to set a court date.

⌒

I was in the swimming pool with John Henry one Saturday afternoon. Loss had accumulated on my shoulders. They slumped and felt heavy, no matter how I tried to hold them back and tell myself I was all right, that I could do this, that this was the right thing. I was so sad. Though I vehemently believed in my reasons for doing what I was doing, and for desiring the change that I did, I knew dragging it all into a courtroom was wrong and it was creating an emotional sinkhole in me. I had to change something, because all the fight I had in my body was being spent going back and forth with John Henry's father. And I knew he wasn't going to budge because he doesn't, as a general rule. That's probably my most and least favorite thing about him. Because I knew that, and I felt the life slipping out of me as a result of the daily grind of phone calls and emails with my attorney about the matter, my wheels started to spin about how not to do it anymore because I couldn't. Not for one more day. My spirit couldn't stand the idea of trashing my son's father in a courtroom because we couldn't agree on where our son should live. I knew he needed his energy and resources for all of the same things I did. There had to be a better way to navigate the raising of this child whom we both love so very much. This child for whom we both want the best. This child who is, unfortunately, not exempt from our respective agendas. This child who sees and feels it all.

"Well, I have a compromise in mind," he said when I called him that Saturday afternoon to ask if there might be a way we could reach one and not allow a judge to make this very important decision about our son's life when we were so much more capable of doing such a thing. I almost dropped the phone.

I guess with all the hard thinking I'd been doing about it, I had conjured him from the pool. When I looked at my phone after getting back to the locker room to change John Henry and myself out of our wet swimsuits, there were several text messages about scheduling his time with our son. We have that connection whether either of us likes to admit it. He is a soul mate to me in terms of what I understand a soul mate really is—one who teaches you something you need to learn and then probably exits in one way or another. John Henry's father has taught me many things. Things about artistry, things about love, and things about children. A lot of people are warm to the touch and cold at the center. He is the opposite. I am very far from perfect, but I have pretty good instincts most of the time. I don't think I would've had a child with a person who didn't have warmth at his center. He has made mistakes like we all have, but does his best with our boy, this boy we share, this boy who connects us forever despite our unease, despite the profound hurt we caused each other.

"It's time I took a shift."

That was not what I was expecting to hear. I had grown so used to the cacophony, the parade of put-downs, the him-versus-me all squared up against what we were supposed to be concentrating on—our son—that I couldn't respond right away. I asked him for a few days to think about it. I called my sister first. I called my therapist second.

"Sissy, I think this is the right thing. You have to have a break. It's killing you to do all of this by yourself for so long. He's getting so big. I'm worried about you. This is the right thing. I feel it."

I knew she was right. My physical weariness was rivaled only by the high level of emotional fatigue I'd reached that summer. I exercised all the time to try to combat the wear-down and to increase my strength and energy, but I felt sore and weak. I ratcheted up my search for spiritual answers to everything in my life. I meditated and journaled to keep an eye on what was happening emotionally—if I didn't, my feelings would slip away and I would become blank or arbitrarily angry, just too tired to keep an emotion present or a thought about why I was having it in my head. Life in general, not just autism, had caught up with me. I was completely on edge and fractious.

When I presented the idea of this proposed shift change to my therapist, she immediately responded that it was time, that we had to try it.

"Barring major trauma, the bond between parent and child is solidified by the time they reach five years old, despite cognitive disorders. I've seen you with John Henry. You're ingrained in him. You need a break. You've got to take one."

I was immediately worried John Henry would think I was abandoning him, that he wouldn't understand where I'd gone, that he would think I didn't want him anymore. Was he going to comprehend what I said to him about such a change? Even if he did, would he care about the reasons? I would cry every time I thought those thoughts, and I thought those thoughts every time I thought of even considering the new arrangement. How could I even contemplate it? I asked myself. This was not in the plan. This was not what a good mother does. This was ultimately selfish. This simply would not do. This was also what I knew I *had* to do. I knew everyone was right—those who'd glimpsed the situation up close knew I had to do something to reclaim some space and let his father take over for a while; after all, John Henry does have two parents.

～

I called his father back almost forty-eight hours later and told him I'd consider it. The idea was that I could leave New York and relocate to Nashville with H. the following May and that John Henry could spend summers with us. He would then spend what is the traditional school year in New York with his father. I would be free to see him as much as I wanted during that time, but I would also be free to attend to myself again—to shore up my career in a way that I hadn't been able to since John Henry was born, to, most importantly, set life up for us in a long-term sense, in a place I knew we could stay probably forever, because make no mistake, he would be coming back to me sooner rather than later.

I hated the idea of a shift change with a purple passion despite the break it presented to me, but it at least let some air into life. I began to visualize what summers might be like: playtime before and after breakfast, no sensory-nightmare walk to school every morning, therapy done at home, outings in the community, swimming in friends' pools, walks at the nature preserve and botanical garden, space for running and jumping, concentrated and actual quality time rather than constant maintenance time, at home with my boy. A fenced yard! A washer and dryer! I began to visualize what the rest of the year might be like. I wasn't sure I could do it. I wasn't sure I could live through how badly I knew I'd miss him in those spaces between every other weekend and holiday breaks. Couldn't I just keep on doing what I was doing? Couldn't I? I told myself that I could, but I also told myself that something had to change, and that this change, this shift change, was the answer for now. Just for now. I kept telling myself, *just for now*, like everything else, *just for now*. Everything changes, it always does, this will be Just. For. Now. What is, is not what will always be.

൚

We came to an agreement. I would take the entire summer. I would create a home team of therapists and be hands-on 24/7. John Henry would return to New York City after Labor Day to resume his regular schedule at his regular school and live under his father's roof for a while. Who knew for how long? The leap I was taking was the biggest of my life. And I knew, for a lot of reasons, that it was necessary that I jump. It was necessary that all of us did.

John Henry's dad and I separated when he was two years old. I've been the full-time parent 75 percent of the time since then. It was time to correct that now, with

John Henry nearing ten, with things happening in a developmental way that indicated a need for more consistent male energy and guidance. Our relationship felt blurry. Was I his mama, his therapist, his nurse, his caregiver, all of the above? Yes, I was all of those things and it didn't feel like the healthiest situation for either of us. I knew John Henry knew how to play on my emotions. I knew I did for him things he could've done for himself. I suppose most mothers find themselves in that situation, but I was becoming more and more conflicted about the nursing part—some things in the area of self-care felt inappropriate for us both. I knew I had to back away. I had to get some distance between us and what we'd become, which was, in some ways, in a relationship that felt dysfunctional at times. He knew no boundaries with me. He touched and grabbed at my breasts, he walked or stomped on my feet with the result of a stress fracture in the right one—I had no ability to draw a demarcation between us. I am a woman. I had to remind myself of that constantly. He is a growing, preadolescent young man. It was no longer appropriate for him to pull back the shower curtain when I was bathing. It was no longer okay for him to see my naked breasts or bottom. It was no longer fine for me to be so familiar with what was happening below his own waistband.

I also knew that I had controlled the relationship between him and his father, as much as I hated to admit it. I had walked the earth for almost nine years feeling like I was the only person on the planet who could take care of our child in the way that he needed. Some of that is natural, for I am his mother and a lot of mothers operate under that notion, but some of that is the result of my damage and my desire to do everything to the letter to keep the world from falling apart on me again. I realized that I had kept John Henry all to myself, mostly due to those fears. I hadn't allowed anyone besides therapists and the occasional babysitter to care for him—I was too nervous—I was convinced that I was the only one he needed. I was wrong. He does need me and he needs me a lot, but he also needs others. He especially needs his father.

I looked forward to summer. I also dreaded the absence that would hit me in the face after it was over.

&

Relocating to Nashville had been my long-term plan for a while and we'd been lucky enough to have already found a home there, so our transition was pretty easy. John Henry already knew all the areas of the house, from his bedroom, to the kitchen, to the living room where he upended the sofa cushions and built forts on almost a nightly basis just like he did with the one in the NYC apartment, to the guest room he loved to hang out in where our resident ghost, whom I'd named Helen, hung out. He knew the fenced front yard and porch swing. He knew the backyard and exactly where the inflatable pool would be set up. He was comfortable and seemed to like stretching out a bit. I'd put together a wonderful team composed of two of the therapists who had worked with him when he was first diagnosed years ago, and a highly recommended music therapist. We started our summer home program June 1. Speech therapy first thing in the morning every weekday, music therapy after lunch three days a week, hippotherapy twice per week, and ABA and life skills every afternoon for four hours. I was determined that he not only wouldn't lose any skills, but that he'd gain some, especially in the executive functioning department.

I got to be with him all day, every day. For seven years, he'd gone to school Monday through Friday, so to be together every Monday through Sunday was new for him and for me. I think we both liked it, mostly. He still got bored from time to time, I still lost patience here and there, and the fragmented segments of time that made up our days sometimes felt too heavy, like I was expecting him to accomplish something game-changing inside one of them because he wasn't breathing urban air. He didn't, not all at once. But he held on to his sign language and developed more willingness to use his talker iPad with Proloquo (an app that facilitates communication) on it, navigating it and communicating with it successfully when motivated. He maintained his self-care routine and I even increased his bathroom interval to every fifty-five minutes from forty-five, which also gave us all a little more space between timer beeps. We worked on keeping his hands down in stores and by the end of the summer he wasn't grabbing candy and biting into it before I could stop him every single time we stood by a checkout counter, but rather learning to carefully consider and choose items and place them in the basket to be purchased. He grew, seemingly nonstop, more into his 90th percentile height and weight status. He got to run in the park with no one holding his hand. He got to play barefoot in the creek. He got to ride horses twice a week and enjoyed it until he figured out it was actually work disguised as fun. He swam almost every day.

Sometimes I would watch him from the breakfast room window and feel the minutes dwindling. *This is it*, I would think to myself. *This is the last seamless summer. From now on, he'll come home to Nashville instead of this being where he lives. It'll be like he's away at boarding school.* I talked myself into thinking of it that way. And in a way, I wasn't lying. I knew there was not yet a truly equivalent school for him in Nashville and no way to get him enough of what he needs under one roof. And New York wasn't enough of what I need. I reminded myself that the time had come for him to be with his father more. I wasn't wrong about that, but if I could've flayed myself to demonstrate my guilt to the world, I probably would've, while simultaneously telling myself and everyone else that it was the right, and the only, thing to do.

⌒

Some couldn't quite believe that I'd made such a decision. I had to smile past the astonished faces when I told certain people about the new arrangement we'd made. They thought they knew me. They thought they knew John Henry. They thought they knew his father. They didn't.

They didn't have any idea how his father had always, to the best of his ability to do so, shown up to do his bit and earnestly wanted to do more. Most folks just didn't know anything about any of it, nor should they have, I guess, but the tendency to judge something one knows nothing about tends to be a quality that exists abundantly in most human beings. We never know a situation unless we're in it. I found myself trying to explain it to people who deserved no such explanation, trying to defend myself against disapproving eyes that had absolutely no clear picture of what our lives were like, trying to put on a brave face and say over and over, "It'll be all right and this is the right thing and it's just for now" when I was dying inside, wondering if what we'd decided was actually the right thing. I was stupidly clamoring for approval and reassurance because I wasn't quite giving it to myself. I was afraid. Afraid of letting go, afraid of making a mistake, afraid of everything about it. In early September, while swimming at the home of one of my best and most supportive friends, a mutual acquaintance nearly laughed in my face when I told her what was about to happen. I decided then and there that I was done explaining. I owed no one justification for this decision. I owed that to no one but my son, and I knew he would never ask me for such a thing. I knew we were good with each other. I made my peace with it that night as Leelee, who had come to be with us for the weekend—just because she is my best friend and a great mother and also someone who understood how hard it was going to be for me to let him leave—and I talked ourselves into slumber, side by side in the same bed just like we used to sleep when we were teenagers and something heavy had happened.

~

The Sunday before Labor Day, the day he was leaving, arrived the following morning. I woke with tears on my face. But I rose early as always and made John Henry's favorite breakfast. We played outside in the inflatable pool that he loves so much. We swung on the front-porch swing. We sprayed the water hose in the front yard and made mudholes. We took a drive, one of his favorite, most calming activities. We had sushi for dinner, another of his favorites. I let him soak in the tub for as long as we had time for after his bath. The minutes ticked away and my stomach grew tighter with each one's disappearance. I packed his backpack, asking him which lunch box he wanted to take to school this year, making sure to keep a smile on my face and my voice light. I still had the one with the planets and stars and the monogram in red that he'd used for the past few years, but had bought another one in plain royal blue with a red zipper and different kind of monogram, thinking he might like something more plain, something more grown-up looking. He pointed to the new, solid blue one when I asked him to choose between the two and I slipped it into the front pocket, just as I always had every morning when we got ready to go to school, along with a few Mardi Gras beads and a couple of squiggly worms. His father texted. He was just a few minutes away. My friends (my other best friend, Traci, had shown up too—I am a fortunate woman) lingered in the kitchen talking, giving us space. I helped John Henry into his sandals. We put his two iPads—one for play and one for talking—in his backpack and walked to the front porch. He ran onto the sidewalk and I ran out after him, skipping and jumping and soaking up his joy that is so very big when he experiences it. I told him we could do it. I put my hands around his waist, bent at the knees, and said, "One-two-three!" He jumped up and wrapped his very long legs around my waist.

"John . . . Henry, John Henry, John Henry, John Henry, John Henry, John Henry, John Henry. John Henry, John Henry, John Henry, John Henry, John Henry, John Henry, John Henry. John Henry, John Henry, John Henry, John Henry, John Henry, John Henry, John Henry. John Henry, John Henry, John Henry, John Henry, John Henry, John Henry, John Henry."

My knees almost buckled. My shoulders ached even as I could tell he was trying to lift himself off of me, trying to help me do this thing that we both needed to do. Tears came. I kept singing his song to him. I. Did. Not. Want. To. Let. Him. Go.

His father arrived and walked through the gate singing, "John Henry!" the way that *he* does. The three of us walked to the porch to get John Henry's backpack. I wrapped my arms around my son and unsuccessfully fought back my tears, told him I loved him, and said I'd see him in a few weeks. His dad took his hand. They turned, went down the porch steps, took the sidewalk together, and passed through the front gate to the street.

I watched them until he was out of my sight. Despite my urge to run with them, to tell them I'd go back to New York, to say this was wrong, to say I'd do anything not to let him think for one second I was making this choice because I wanted to, I let him go. I whispered to the crickets, to the air, to the sky, to the stars, to myself, to God, to him, "I love you, sweet boy."

I turned to go back inside and sang softly to myself.

"John . . . Henry, John Henry, John Henry, John Henry, John Henry, John Henry, John Henry.

"John Henry, John Henry, John Henry, John Henry, John Henry, John Henry, John Henry.

"John Henry, John Henry, John Henry, John Henry, John Henry, John Henry, John Henry.

"John Henry, John Henry, John Henry, John Henry, John Henry, John Henry, John Henry."

The Day We Went to the Moon

He was home for the long Presidents' Day weekend in February. I flew up to New York on the Friday to get him, having had to continuously bat back my anxiety during the days before over not having seen him for two and a half weeks. I'd gotten home from a run of shows that Monday with a bad case of flu, but as life doesn't stop, neither did I. I kept going, trying to rest in between tasks, errands, and my lists of to-dos and shoulds, all the while feeling physically vulnerable, which always sends my emotions into overdrive and results in what I call "mental doughnuts." It's as if my mind is a car in a vacant parking lot and I'm the driver who has gone completely out of control, laughing maniacally while holding the gas pedal down to the floor and the steering wheel all the way to the right. I spin, spin, and spin with the what-ifs of the day. *How, what, when, where, and who? Is he okay?*

How, what, when, where, and who? Is he okay? How, what, when, where, and who? Nothing would soothe me until I got him in sight, until I could touch his hand and ruffle his hair, until I knew that he was okay.

The shift change had been good, though hard. After nine and a half years of being his primary caregiver most of the time, I suddenly wasn't that person during the spaces between every other weekend. My body didn't know how to process such a change. Even though I was thankful for the chance to rest a bit, I was still somehow on high alert. Where was he? *Oh yes, he's with his father, he's fine, he's in New York, he's in school, where he needs to be. Everything is fine. Everything is fine. Everything is fine!* I'd tell myself even as I fought back the painful waves that washed over my center every time I thought of him and the fact that he was not with me. He was not in his room. He was not on an outing with his teacher. He was away from me for the first time in his life. I had let him go back to New York with his father. I had let him go. I was still watching and listening, but mostly from afar. I had let him go. I had *had* to let him go, in a way, for a bit.

I'd send a text message every morning when I knew they were getting ready for school.

"How is the boy today?"

"How's mister doing?"

If it was the weekend, I'd ask,

"What are the plans for Saturday?"

I'd watch the clock and send another text as soon as I knew they'd had time to get home from school.

"How's John Henry?"

"How was his day?"

"I haven't gotten a note from school yet—is everything okay?"

His father was kind to always reply, and even apologized when it took him longer than he knows he'd like to wait for a response from me if he were sending the text message. I always told him that it's no problem—I understand the need for both hands to be available for the job at hand and for them not to be busy text messaging. I understand the race to get out the door on time in the mornings with a charged iPad and a packed lunch box in the backpack. I understand it all. He also seemed to understand my need to know that everything was all right. When you can't talk to your child, you depend on the other parent to tell you the state of things—is he eating well, is he sleeping okay, how are his executive functioning skills coming along, what did they say at school beyond the note that we get every day? The tether is always attached, but the degree to which it is depends on others—send me a photo, send him this video of me talking to him, show him this photograph of our dog, tell him only two more nights to sleep until I'm there . . .

Work filled much of my time after he went back to New York. A book release, a record release, traveling, touring, talking, singing—I guess I was trying to make up for what felt to the career part of my life like lost time. I knew it hadn't been lost time in my general life, I knew that I'd been doing a very important job while I was, I guess, what you would call kind of away, despite my best efforts to not be. The world at large doesn't really seem to consider motherhood an actual job that takes up time and energy, only something that should be done seamlessly, perfectly, according to outside subscription, and completely willfully done even without notice or gratitude from others. Those of us who choose to do other things with our lives in addition to being mothers must fight for space and equality in the workplace and in the eyes of the world. It also seems to be a given that motherhood is more important than fatherhood, and the idea that there must be something wrong with—or even missing or broken in—women who choose to allow someone else to take up the slack every once in a while is still freely thrown about. That isn't the book I'm writing, however, except to say that when we are forced to choose between our work and our families, it is never an easy choice to make and we always resent having to make it. I wondered often if John Henry's father felt the same anxiety I did during the years that came before, before we made this shift change. He stayed in touch, but didn't text me three or more times per day to check in. He didn't have to know every little thing like I try to do. I am jealous of his ease about it all. I am also determined to stay as connected as I can, however I can, every single day. Is that just a mother's way? I don't know, but it's mine.

⌒

I left the house in Nashville at 4 a.m. that Friday. It was so cold, I gasped as I walked out onto the front porch and toward the gate at the end of the walkway, carrying only my tote that held a few of my daily essentials—my wallet, some basic cosmetics, a phone charger, my emergency nerve-settling pills, a notebook, my iPad, a book to read, plus a change of clothes and some gummy bears for the plane ride back. I'd get the rest of what we needed for our travels when I got to the city. I climbed into the back seat of my preordered Uber and headed to the airport, silently sending him telepathic messages all the way. *I'm on my way, baby. I'll see you at school, sweet boy. No more sleeps, my angel.* I'd been in tears for days, and that morning felt like a long time coming.

I looked down at the cityscape from the plane window and felt no nostalgia for the life I had lived in New York, only the ratcheting up of my heart rate, and thought only of the countdown of hours until I saw my boy and what possible state LaGuardia's Terminal B would be in when we returned together that afternoon to wait for our plane back to Tennessee. I landed at LaGuardia at 9 a.m. I made my way to Manhattan, had coffee with a friend, then a late breakfast with my agent, Laura. I always insist on taking the earliest flight—if it gets delayed or canceled there is a much better chance of still getting there on time to pick him up from school, something I never want to miss doing when I can. I also shudder at the thought of having to tell his father I'm not going to make it on time—he hadn't ever understood my need to leave New York and made me feel a fool every time we discussed it and the details of my not living there, as if only a hillbilly of the lowest order wouldn't want to try to sustain herself in the supposed greatest place on earth. When I go back, I do try to make the most of it—I see friends, I stop by my old haunts—the stationery store on Eighth Street that might hold a magic notebook, pen, or sweet card for someone I love; or the French restaurant on Grove that always feels like an escape to somewhere softer and kinder. I made a few more stops here and there to kill time, then in the midafternoon, I started the familiar walk through our old neighborhood to his school to pick him up. We always take a late afternoon flight out.

I walked in the door and told the receptionist I was ready for him—I'd prearranged for his teachers to have him ready to fly. I took a seat on the small green bench just inside the two sets of double doors that simultaneously provide entry for and protection from the world and waited for him to be accompanied down the stairs. I pulled out my phone and requested another Uber to take us to the airport.

Isn't it funny how we recognize the footsteps of those with whom we are familiar? Maybe it's just my ear, but I know who's approaching by the way their feet fall on the floor. Some shuffle, some stomp, some clomp. I know, even though my son is constantly growing and changing, how his feet land, and I listened for them as I sat and thought about how he couldn't come down the stairs fast enough.

Clomp, clomp, clomp, and a little bit of verbalization—he was on his way. My eyes filled with tears as I waited for him and his teacher to descend to the bottom of the staircase and then around the railing to where I sat. He saw me and looked surprised, even though I'd sent a video to his father the day before to tell him that I was on my way. He sat down on my lap. He put his arm around my neck. He pressed his lips to my cheek. He took my face in his hands to turn it directly toward his and he smiled. My heart grew again, as he has always made it do, and my tears flowed. I sang a few lines of one of his songs to him. He sang a few back to me.

Me: *Da da da da da da da, da da da da da da*
JH: *da DA da da, da da da da da da . . .*

The *how, what, when, where, and who* eased. He was okay. I probably touched his hand twenty times during the ride to the airport. He pulled it away but slyly smiled in my direction every time. There is part of him that seems to understand my need to get my mama touches in—the hair smoothing, the shirt straightening, the hand in the space between his shoulder blades—though he's still typical enough for it all to annoy him at least a little. "Mamaaaaaa . . ." I imagine him saying as he shrugs out from under the palm I'm always placing on his shoulder.

I'd stopped by Whole Foods to get his favorite snacks for the plane: three packages of ten pieces of prosciutto-wrapped mozzarella cheese. Though he is older and less rambunctious now, I still never get on a plane with him without being fully prepared with my arsenal of tools:

plenty of food, a big bottle of water, candy to dole out one piece at a time for bargaining for good behavior, a fully charged backup iPad should the two that belong to him run out of juice or somehow otherwise malfunction, a full-size pack of wipes, Mardi Gras beads, a magazine filled with photographs of water—oceans, lakes, pools, whatever I can find that I know he'll like to look at. We flew through the air as he watched his iPad, wireless headphones on his head, and ate twenty-three prosciutto rolls. It was one of his near-perfect flights. I remembered the years that I fretted so much over his diet. I thought about how I don't anymore, but that I would be making his dreaded Mama Popsicles that weekend—those that I concoct from organic no-sugar-added juice and supplements and then pour into molds so that he can at least get some nutrients in his system if he's going to eat ten Popsicles per day. I think about how to get broccoli extract into his diet. I've tried before but it tastes like soap and is detectable in the amount that they say might make a difference. Even my son, who is sort of famous for his healthy appetite, rejects it, even in a Mama Popsicle, and this is a child who requests things like sushi and cucumbers with feta cheese.

We landed happily in Nashville without incident. H. picked us up outside of baggage claim. He'd had the flu too, but rallied and made the trip to the airport so John Henry and I didn't have to wait on an Uber or a taxi. Waiting is something we don't do if we don't have to. It can make life feel like a military operation—I calculate travel and wait times down to the minute if I can and do my best to make it all run on schedule while keeping my eyes peeled for family restrooms and potential perils all around us. It was dark outside but John Henry smiled and looked out the window in the back seat as we traveled on Interstate 40 toward home. We arrived, got out of the car, went through the front gate, and my sweet boy set himself loose in the front yard for some twirls. His yard, his front porch, and his swing. He was happy. So was I. *Is he okay?* Yes.

After he twirled for a few minutes, I talked him into the house so we could settle in for the evening. During the time he'd been gone I purchased a new chair for the living room. He noticed it immediately and sat down in it, eyeing the leopard print of the upholstery, a jolt of pattern into our mostly visually quiet home. I like to keep things calm, even for our eyes. I asked him if he liked the new chair while he first curled himself into a ball to fit into it, then stood up, lifted the seat cushion, and sat down again. A new fort.

Since he ate so many snacks on the plane, dinner was a nonevent. He enjoyed a bath in the big tub in the master bathroom, snuggled into his pajamas and then his bed. I lay down beside him while he watched a movie. I tried not to keep my hand on him because I know it annoys him, but it is always hard to resist. He doesn't seem to need reassurance that he is really home, but I always do. *He is here. He is safe in his bed. He will be here in the morning. He is okay.* H. woke me after we'd both fallen asleep. I got up and plugged the iPad and headphones into their chargers. A nightly ritual.

The weekend went by as days normally do when he's at home. We rise early, usually before 7 a.m., to start our day. Sometimes I wake to the sounds John Henry makes in the morning—some days he'll lie in bed for a while before he gets up, and some mornings he'll jump up and start walking around the house, even going to the refrigerator and getting out milk or juice—but now and then I make it out of bed before he does and get to start breakfast without feeling like I'm behind. Whenever we do meet, we make our way to the bathroom, then the timer is set so we can stay on schedule. I make his favorite breakfasts—cinnamon rolls, bacon, sausage, boiled eggs, cheese toast—whatever I can think of that he likes, he gets. I am fully aware that I spoil him, but so what? He may not be able to tell me that he wants a cheeseburger with his voice, but I'll go to every length to make sure he can request one somehow if he does want one, even if it's by him seeing hamburger meat in the refrigerator and bringing it to me, usually shoving it under my nose or dropping it into my hands. I actually like it when he does that—there's no mistaking what he wants and it's his most natural way of communicating what he wants to me. Plus, it always makes me laugh. The problem, of course, is if he wants something he doesn't see. I worry about what he would like to have that he can't tell me about, what he would like to have that I miss, so I reinforce his physical requests by finding the icon on the iPad and showing him where it is. He seems annoyed by it sometimes. I would be too. If what I indicated wasn't honored and I was made to say it over and over again for practice, I'd probably be frustrated. But we do it to reinforce and encourage. That's what we're supposed to do.

I got all of his favorite snacks from Costco—they have the prized prosciutto-wrapped mozzarella rolls in a three-pack, which saves some money. The inflatable hot tub in the backyard has been filled and heating for a few days so it's ready for splashing and swimming. It's cold outside so we keep a fire going in the living room. He is home and my heart feels better. We are peaceful. I am mostly relaxed.

But only mostly. A sense of anxiety hovers around me because I know if I'm not watching him every minute—and what person could do that when there are always other things to do at the same time—accidents are bound to happen. That isn't abnormal—every parent knows that there are times at which one must throw up her hands and accept that reality—but the sense of chaos is ratcheted up in our house. There is no reasoning that can be done nor cause and effect or consequence of action that can be consistently successfully explained. For example: Since John Henry can now open the door to the master bathroom and turn on the water in the tub, he will sneak to the back of the house, open the door, throw back the shower curtain, and turn the water on full blast all by himself. He always remembers to take off his pants and underwear before he gets in, but not his shirt as a general rule, which I don't quite understand. I try to let him take as many baths as he wants because why not? But when he gets away from me and starts one on his own, I worry that it's dangerous, and not only because he could scald himself with too-hot water (though he always tests the temperature with his foot before he gets in) or fall, but because he also sometimes forgets that various equipment isn't water resistant. Expensive wireless headphones and iPads know no special treatment. He's drowned so many of each, I've lost count. That was the case again, when I got distracted talking to my friend Savannah, who had dropped by for a visit on Saturday evening. As we talked, I suddenly noticed that John Henry had left the room and tuned my hearing toward the back of the house to the faint sound of water running. I ran to the bathroom and, sure enough, his headphones, the ones he depends on for lessening his hearing sensitivity and wears almost all the time, were floating in the water. I fished them out but they were too far gone. Savannah put them in a Ziploc bag of rice to see if that trick would work, but I knew it wouldn't. I just picked up my phone and ordered a new pair that would be delivered two days later. I had a cheap backup pair in his closet that would have to fill the space in between. File all of that under the cost of this whole thing, I guess. After my heart stopped pounding I wondered about the other costs of this disorder besides the financial ones—ragged nerves, tattered cells. I sighed, then laughed it off and kept going. I prepared him a plate of pork tenderloin and risotto and set it on the table so we could eat dinner when he was through with the early evening soak he decided to take.

There's always a shenanigan, always a bit of a mess to clean up, always something to manage. I think of my mama friends and how their lives are so different from mine—generally they can tell their children to do something and it's done—*put on your shoes, pick up your toys, tell me about your day at school.* I know nothing of that life, for the most part. But I know *our* life very well by now. I know our routines, and I know how to (mostly) keep things running smoothly. The surprises, however, still surprise me.

Monday morning brought sunshine and plans for a haircut for John Henry followed by a trip to the YMCA to go swimming. He doesn't like sitting still for a haircut, or for much of anything, but we get them anyway. I take him to my stylist, who has a son of her own who's just a year older than mine so she gets it, at least, on some level. She's sweet and encouraging, always praising how well my boy does when he sits in her chair. And he did do well! He sat through the entire fifteen-minute procedure without getting up until the last snip of the scissors, almost. That's okay. We do what we have to, to get it all done, and our sweet Kristin follows him around the shop to get any stray strawberry-blond tendrils that she missed. There are so many angels in our lives.

When his hair was trimmed, we said goodbye, and instead of going to the playground to swing on the swing set like we normally do after a haircut, I announced that I'd packed our suits and towels and that we'd be going swimming instead. A quick stop by Sonic for some Tater Tots for him and a Diet Coke for me—I love stopping by Sonic because when I pull up to place an order I always look back to ask him what he'd like and he always makes the signs for *eat* and *drink*, which thrills me to no end—*he's generalizing, he always remembers*—and we made our way to the YMCA.

We changed in the family restroom. At this point, I know people look at me funny and are possibly uncomfortable when I take him into a women's restroom so I try to avoid it. I also get it—he's a big fellow and I might question his presence among half- or completely naked women too if I didn't know what I was seeing. I try to see us as another would and try to accommodate what is considered normal, though I can't always do that. I do always breathe a sigh of relief when I find an unoccupied restroom meant for those who need assistance and a slightly agitated one when I see a seemingly wholly healthy person come out of one when we've been waiting. I am thankful that the one designated for families at the Y is mostly always free.

I've been practicing finding ways to change into my swimsuit so that he doesn't see me unclothed. I don't know how he processes what he sees, so I'm creative with how to hold a towel and how to cover myself while changing in the same room as him. I try to respect his privacy and hone his sense of propriety as well. Again, not easy, as he seems to sometimes be quite happy to prance around with no pants on, but we're getting there. I put on

my one-piece and long-sleeve surfing shirt. I slipped my
feet into a pair of pool slides. I helped him shed his street
clothes in exchange for his swimming gear. Though the
swimming pool is indoors, it's always a bit cool and we
both need extra layers. We walked to the pool.

I panicked a little when I saw that it was crowded.
There was a seniors water aerobics class starting up. Most
people are nice, but some, particularly those who don't
have as much to do as others or those who either never
knew or have forgotten what it's like to have children,
aren't. They want to know why he acts the way he does,
why I have to watch him like I do, or why I don't dis-
cipline him in the way that they would, or think they
would. We thankfully encountered no such people on
this early Monday afternoon, only seemingly kind women
who found us, probably, weird but in need of their understanding and silence. Another parent played with his two
boys in the portion of the pool they'd roped off from the
aerobics class. I tried to keep the constant stream of snot
from John Henry's nose from going into the water to not
much avail.

He suddenly got still. He hadn't been to the bathroom
that morning, and I sensed that it was time. I told him we
needed to go back to the restroom. He took the hand that
I held out, surprisingly complied with my instructions (it's
sometimes quite difficult to convince him to get out of the
water), and got out of the pool. We returned to the family
restroom, and I'll be damned if my instincts weren't right.
Lo and behold, the eagle landed.

I was beside myself with happiness. It was a ground-breaking moment. I live in fear of ill-timed bowel movements, especially in public spaces, so the idea that we might one day not have to worry about them so much feels like a glimpse of a life that might be less stressful than the one we have now. That's a line to be straddled, though. Parenting is building, this block on top of that one. Everything we do is for both the present and the future, but it's important to stay in the moment and appreciate any day that any of the pieces fit together. At that moment I could've done cartwheels across a football field in celebration. John Henry stared at me while I smiled and repeated how proud I was of him. I probably high-fived him twelve times. I sang, I did a happy dance. He jumped up and down a few times—I assume, for joy. I trust, in honor of himself and the hard work he's been doing for so long. I didn't know if something clicked with him or if we just got lucky on the timing, but I also didn't care. We went back to the pool to finish our swim. I was relieved. I didn't have to worry about it happening again for thirty whole minutes while he splashed and swam. Life was good.

When it was time to go home, we went back to the restroom and got out of our swimming clothes and into the ones we'd worn there. I told him I had to stop by the store and that we'd get him something special, that he could pick out anything he wanted. I never know how appropriate it is to make a big deal out of these things—it is normal for a boy to go to the bathroom where it is acceptable to go, but we've struggled so hard and so long over it that now that it is happening with more regularity, I want him to know what a difference it makes in his life. He may not think like that, but what do I have to go by? I'd rather err on the side of commemorating every success. The one we had that day was no small thing.

I held his hand in the drugstore. We made our way to the school supply aisle for a three-sectioned notebook with a red cover for me—one section is always reserved for John Henry business—and then to the toy aisle for him to pick out his reward. He chose a small, squishy yellow ball with tentacles all over it. We already had two just like it at home that I'd gotten for him earlier in the week but that was okay. I asked him if that was what he wanted, and as he carefully scanned the shelves for something else, he held on to the ball. We made our way to the checkout.

A kindly older gentleman was behind the counter. My heart rate rose, because checkout lanes are always a danger zone. There is candy to grab and bite into and though we're always working on not doing that it's still very much a possibility. There are other small items that can be popped into a small mouth and destroyed quicker than I can say, "Hands by your sides, John Henry, don't touch anything."

"Out of school today, I see?"

"Yes, sir, we're out for the long weekend."

"Where do you go to school, young man?"

"He goes to school in New York City."

I could see him out of the corner of my eye, intensely staring at the rolls of Life Savers and the boxes of Tic Tacs.

"There's a school there that can better give him what he needs than any I've found here."

"Well, I was the attorney for the special education district in the Memphis school system for many years."

"I am quite familiar with . . . NO! John Henry . . ."

He had picked up and bitten through a roll of Mentos.

"No. Give those to me."

I took the Mentos away, put them in the bag that held the notebook and the squishy ball, and fished a five-dollar bill out of my wallet while holding John Henry's hand.

"Can you ring them up without scanning them? I'm afraid to let him see them again."

"You just take those."

"We have to pay."

"No, you do not. And you bring him back here anytime you want to."

Fearing more havoc, I thanked the sweet cashier while trying not to cry out of gratitude and frustration and steered John Henry out of the store and into the back seat of the car. I got in behind the wheel, then I looked back at him through my tears and laughed while he jiggled his new ball.

I think about those smug "My child is on the honor roll" bumper stickers and how much they annoy me. I would like to have a bumper sticker touting *my* child's accomplishments. I am so proud of my boy. Maybe my ego is wrapped up in how he does, just like those parents who seem to base their worth in what sort of grades their children get; maybe his accomplishments mean that I'm not failing. Maybe it also means that I will be able to let go, even if only in some small ways.

We're not perfect, and we never will be, but some days we're more perfect than others. Some days he shows me a light at the end of my tunnel. And some days he shows me I'm not in a tunnel at all, and that I'm just in life, our life, as crazy and chaotic as it can be. A life in which going to the bathroom appropriately and being welcomed instead of shamed inside a store feels like being shot out of a rocket and landing in some sort of beautiful outer space—a space where we don't have to worry about people getting mad at us because we're different. Every now and then, we find a space where we can celebrate our successes, no matter how small others might think they are. A space where low impulse control is understood. A space in which I don't do mental doughnuts. A space where *how, what, when, where, and who* doesn't seem so hard to figure out.

Dream #3

Your voice sounds like it does when we're awake—lilting, soft, sweet, yet boyish and quietly authoritative. You ask questions but are certain at the same time, not of the answers, but of the solidity of mystery. Your knowing that our waking world's definitions of truth are too slippery for anyone to hold on to is as bright as a springtime sky and as heavy as midnight. You appear to want to confirm, but I sense you are artfully reminding me through your questions.

I thought for a second that it could've been real. I thought about how we'd talked. I thought about your voice and I lay there, trying to burn the sound into my brain so that I wouldn't forget it. How could I forget it? I never do. But still I went over it again and again as my tears fell and I let go, little by little, of the hope that you might say something when you opened your eyes.

Maybe it won't be today. But I know the day will come in whatever way that it does. To that, I hold on.

This Part Is the Worst Part

"Oh, honey."

I'd heard him start to cry after we'd both gone to bed. I gave it a beat to see if maybe he was having a bad dream and had cried out in his sleep, thinking that if he had, he'd settle back down. The cries kept coming. I threw back my covers, went to his room, and sat down beside him on the bed where he lay. He writhed and buried his head in his pillow. I tried to put my arms around him but his body was as stiff as a board.

"What's wrong, baby?"

He sat up. Tears poured down his flushed face, his mouth open in an anguished shape, his eyes terrified. He put his hands over his ears and alternated between flopping down and shrieking into his pillow and trying to stop himself from crying while doing the most heartbreaking thing that children do when something has gone terribly wrong—trying to breathe normally after they've become so upset that the rhythm has gone ragged. His bottom lip quivered as he struggled to reclaim some depth for his shallow, stuttering, double breaths.

I started to cry too, though silently, so maybe he wouldn't know.

I can't stand this part.

This part is the worst part.

This part is a nightmare.

In fact, I hate these moments the most of all the moments I hate. More than the exclusion, more than the staring and misunderstanding of other people, more than the harrowing vision of a future we're unprepared for, more than anything. With all of the helplessness I feel in so many situations, I feel it most intensely in this one. These moments are the ones in which I know the least.

If I am unable to know what's wrong, how can I help? If I am unable to know, then who is able? If no one can figure out what hurts him, where does that leave him? A crying fit can lead my mind from the present moment to a vision of my son abandoned, alone, and hurt in five seconds flat. How the mind spirals. Yes, this part is the worst part.

I went through the list of possible causes in my mind. Is he in physical pain? I stood up and got three chewable ibuprofen from his bathroom cabinet. I tried to get him to take them but he pushed my hand away and refused them. I bit one in half and chewed it up so he might think they were candy. He loves candy. He then took them from my hand, put one to his tongue, and gave them back to me. I put them on his nightstand. I offered him a drink of water but he pushed that away too. I tried everything I could think of—rubbing his back, applying deep pressure to his arms and legs from my hands—I did everything short of getting him out of bed, which didn't seem like a smart move if I wanted to get us back to sleep. It was clear that I couldn't do anything but just be there. So that's what I did.

I lay by his side and wondered—*does he have an ear infection? He's in the water every single day and now his hands are over his ears, particularly the right one. Could just be that he isn't wearing his headphones right now but I know what water in the ear feels like and it hurts like hell. I hope he'll take the ibuprofen. He might when I'm not looking. He could have a headache. A migraine? God, please don't let him have those. A brain tumor? Appendicitis? Is he touching his side? The virus? Growing pains? Leg cramps? I had terrible leg cramps when I was his age. Did he see something on his iPad that scared him or made him sad? Is it the ghost that lives in the guest room? What is he feeling? Is he intuiting something? Is this a delayed reaction to something that happened today? Is he worried about his brother? Is he thinking about me getting mad at him for splashing so much water out of the tub during his bath tonight? It took two towels to mop it all up and he thought it was funny, or he at least laughed when I got angry. Hell, I don't know. All I can do is pray, I guess.*

Please God, please God, please God, please God, please God, let him be okay. Let him settle down and not feel pain. Let me know that he will be okay. Please bring peace and comfort to him. Please. Please.

I know we have to hurt sometimes. I know we all get sick, I know we all have to cry. But not having anyone understand our pain of whatever kind must create a whole separate sort of agony. Does his experience, whatever it is, ever really register as real if he cannot have someone know what it is they're witnessing happen to or within him? I am his witness, yet I don't know what I'm supposed to reflect back to him. I can acknowledge that he's upset, but I don't know how to specifically validate whatever it is that's causing the trouble. I don't know what I'm supposed to have empathy for other than a generalized sense of his pain. That's agonizing for me, and it must be crazy-making for him. How could he help but feel trapped inside his discomfort? This part of experience—the part where another person understands and acknowledges what you're feeling—is something I can't give him.

Oh, my heart.

Oh, his heart.

I read an account the other day of a woman taking her autistic son to a healer of unspecified type. The healer prayed over the boy and told the mother to repeat the mantra "I have a healthy, happy son" until it became so. And apparently, it became so.

I have a healthy, happy son.
I have a healthy, happy son.
I have a healthy, happy son.

I lay there beside him, rubbing his back when he'd let me, telling him it would be all right, prayers and questions squirming against one another in my brain. He started to settle down. He inched closer to me and threw his arm over my upper abdomen, which is a bit out of character for him. He is physically affectionate but in a mostly fleeting manner. He hugs freely, but for only as long as it is his idea. His arm was flung over me and he nestled his head in the hollowed-out spot between my clavicle and breast. I thought I'd start crying again, but held it in and concentrated on holding him. His breathing evened out, his body loosened, and he slipped under the first veil of sleep, turning over as he felt me move my shoulder out from under him. He finally released one deep, extended sigh. I stood up from the bed and let go a sigh of my own, pulled the covers up around his shoulders, and left his room.

I slipped back under my covers, worried and shaken. I thought about mind reading—how much of it we do as human beings, how much communication is unspoken and how much isn't. I can generally know, because my son cries, that he is upset or that something is wrong. I can't specifically know, because I don't understand his language. As much as we work on communication, the subtleties that can never be relayed from touching a photograph with a label on an iPad are endless. Does he even know how much I love him when I can't give him all that he needs or wants? Does he think I'm just ignoring him? I said another prayer that he doesn't, that he would remain asleep, and that peace would cover us.

The Tender Thread

I opened the door to his room at 8:15 a.m. He wasn't in his bed. My heart plummeted to my feet and I called his name.

"John Henry?"

I was shaking from head to toe. During the three seconds it took me to turn around and find him in his pod—a hanging swing in the corner of his bedroom—adrenaline flew through my veins and whooshed in my eardrums. My armpits tingled and my stomach seemed to flip over, sending a wave of nausea up to my throat. I suppose the relatively peaceful summer we'd been having made me think I'd maybe worn out my fight-or-flight mechanism because I hadn't had that feeling in a while, but no, it is still very functional. I guess that's a good thing. I apparently still need it. For managing disasters.

He was naked from the waist down and covered with the furry blanket that provides maximum snuggliness for his downtime. That he was naked wasn't surprising; his disrobing isn't unusual, though I don't always understand its function. It could be comfort, it could be preparation for something like swimming, bathing, or going to the bathroom (and he could've been doing all of those things in his dreams or in his mind, somehow), or it could be a random occurrence—so that didn't bother me so much other than to consider that it isn't ever seemingly of concern to him. What hit me was the realization, indicated to me by my panic, of just how utterly terrified I am that I'm going to lose him or something is going to happen to him. The three seconds that passed between seeing an empty bed and finding him dozing in his pod felt like a total collapse of my world.

～

Sometimes I feel like this is all hanging by a tiny, tender thread—one that is attached to our good intentions but is pulled tense by the weight of us. At the top of the thread is the collection of things that hold our lives together—routine, resources, support, hypervigilance. At the other end of the thread is us—happy, healthy, and together. Beneath us, the blank yet sharp-toothed nothingness of tragedy and grief licks its lips like a greedy monster. The thread struggles to stay intact and could snap at any minute with one little twist in the wrong direction. One little twist and we would be lost.

I try, with what feels like increasing focus, to keep us out of harm's way. Extra locks on doors. Extra checking to make sure gates are latched. With every progression in ability comes another danger. Mastering the turning of a doorknob and opening the door to which it is attached doesn't exactly represent freedom for him or me. While yes, I am happy about his burgeoning maturity and independence, it also reminds me of what might happen if he got on the other side of said door without me.

If I leave the bathroom while he's in the tub, will he stand up to splash water around like he loves to do and fall and hit his head? He has slipped before. Every time, I've been there to catch him, or so I believe. What happens when I'm not there? What happens if I am there at some future moment and he's too big for me to help and he falls on me and we're both hurt?

If he escapes through the front door and gets to the gate before I catch up with him, and someone has forgotten to make sure the gate latched when they went through it, he could be in the middle of the street in seconds. There's a little hill just to the left of our house that's hard to see over. If he managed to get outside the gate and onto the sidewalk alone, what would he do? Would he wander off and get lost, or get picked up by someone with ill intentions, or both? Would he find the nearest body of water, jump in, and drown? Would he wander into the street and get hit by a car? I size up every situation for its list of possibly dangerous scenarios. Nothing and no place is carefree. When we get in the car, I check and double-check.

Are the doors locked? What if he opens the one he's sitting by while we're driving down the road? Is his seat belt fastened? He's already shown that he likes to wiggle out of it and has been putting the shoulder strap behind him for years, despite my protests, so I searched for a guard to work against that. How long until he figures out how to get it off?

With every forward step comes a new risk and the reminder of how very fragile the thread that spans between peace and chaos, safety and hazard, and even life and death really is.

It is not, all in all, a bad thing to worry and look for the next disaster all the time despite the toll it takes. In this case, it is a major part of what keeps us going and keeps that tender thread from snapping. I cannot afford to take my eyes off any of the details for a second lest I get to know the feeling of my heart plummeting to my feet, the feeling I had this morning, on a more permanent basis. That's what I tell myself. But it isn't really true. I'm not really in control of anything despite how I try to prop up the idea that I am. All of the moves I make every day to keep him safe can only do so much and the rest is left up to him and God, because when I've done everything I can think of, I still sometimes lose track of him, even if it's just for three seconds.

I guess no parent that's paying attention would survive without some kind of faith, without at least a modicum of belief that the thread won't snap, otherwise we'd never sleep or do anything but keep our eyes permanently on

our children. No one is capable of that. I heard somewhere that angels exist because children do—someone
has to watch them when their parents can't. Even angels
fall down on the job. All it takes is a second for life to
change forever—the buzz of the phone in the cupholder
next to the driver's seat catches the attention, the step into
the dog pile next to the front gate makes you forget to
ensure it's closed all the way, the not-quite-tight-enough
grip around his wrist lets him break free on a busy sidewalk and bolt into the street.

Snap.

I almost lost him once in an airport. We'd been on vaca-
tion and were flying back to New York. We had to change
planes in Nashville, and he broke away from me as we were
on our way from one gate to another. I was weighed down
with carry-ons, of course, and shouted down the terminal that he was loose and someone needed to catch him.
"Please, someone stop that boy that's running!" No one
paid any attention to us. No one tried to stop him. I guess
he didn't present as anything but a typical five-year-old
and no one thought anything about him running ahead of
his harried mother. Or maybe no one cared though that
certainly can't be true. I finally caught up and stopped him
before anything happened. Those (probably less than) sixty
seconds were terrifying. I didn't know that I would be able
to get to him before he was intercepted by someone or
something that wouldn't take kindly to a wild, hollering

boy who couldn't make understandable words. That part of the fear is sometimes the scariest part of all.

I hear stories all the time about disabled people having outbursts and being misunderstood, then taken into custody of some kind and usually harmed in the process. The older and larger that John Henry gets, the greater my fear of that grows. If he were somehow in a scenario where he was without another person who knows him and could explain, and he grew anxious, and he turned aggressive, I'm sure someone would call the police. He'd be restrained, then possibly thrown into a jail cell because no one would understand what they were seeing or how to deal with a large man who has severe autism, is scared, and is advocating for himself the only way he knows how. The way things are in this world, he could be killed on the spot.

Snap.

.

.

.

I think of my grandmother.

Her daughter was killed by my father. It was a murder-suicide.

I think of my other grandmother, who died ten days after my parents.

I don't know to whom I relate more—the one who has carried the pain of losing a child and has suffered an unspeakable agony for so long, or the one who couldn't stand it and couldn't carry on without her child, knowing the extent of his pain and what the world felt like after he left it. Which one would I be?

They both knew about the tender thread. They both felt it snap. Before it did, had they any idea just how vulnerable it was? Or did they think, did they have faith, that their children could take care of themselves, that the thread would stay intact since they appeared to be functioning and capable adults? Maybe I am more aware of its fragility because my son has so many obstacles to independence present in his life now. Maybe he won't ever be capable of complete self-sufficiency, but the adult part is coming and more quickly than I will know how to handle it. He will soon try to take charge of himself whether he knows he isn't ready to or not. That's human nature. I don't want to take away his independent thought or action. So I work harder at thinking of and locating all the potential perils. I work harder at noticing upticks in behaviors and trying to correct them. Then, what else can I do?

I am always reminding myself to find faith.

To remember faith.

⁓

Early afternoon later in the day, I overheard Kaylee, his ABA teacher, tell him, "No, we don't do that. That hurts me."

He was digging his fingernails into her hand to protest doing his work. I ran through the FBA. Function—to escape. Behavior—physical violence. Assessment—he thinks this is the most efficient way to get out of doing something he doesn't want to do. We encourage him to use the "asking for a break" card. It wasn't handy at the breakfast table where they were sitting, working on utensil use.

I stood up and went toward the room where they were and met them coming toward me.

"Are you okay? Did he scratch you?"

"I'm fine, he just dug his nails in."

"I just cut them this morning. I'm sorry."

I do the math every time this happens. *If this happens with someone who doesn't understand, then they will retaliate or call for help or, or, or . . .*

It's more likely that he will, however unintentionally, hurt himself.

I try to visualize neither scenario, but instead a happy and healthy young man, a happy and healthy grown man, a happy and healthy life.

∽

I'm not in control of anything. All of the moves I make every day to keep him safe can only do so much and the rest is left up to him and God, because when I've done everything I can think of I still sometimes lose track of him, even if it's just for three seconds.

∽

I think of the thread again. I imagine what it must be made of, the part that is holding us to those things we think keep us safe. Strands of hope, trust, courage, mettle, spirit, grit, love, faith—every kind of the most fragile butterflies that are born in the heart. I don't give them enough credit for the work they're doing. The fragile elements are the ones that really matter. They are the things that keep me going back to the routine, resources, support, and hypervigilance. Without them, I couldn't reach down in my guts for the will to do the others every day. The fragile parts are the strongest ones in this mechanism. I must remember to lean on them more.

∽

John Henry, H., and I spent the late afternoon and early evening enjoying a visit with my dear friend Anastasia around her swimming pool. It was lovely, and I even took my work with me, knowing that if there is one place where John Henry is happy and relatively safe, one place where I can breathe a bit easier, it is a body of water with close boundaries. Last summer, in that very pool, he learned to jump in from the side of the deep end. He would shout "E!" every time he did it. Today was the first day we'd been there this year. I kept wondering if he was going to remember how much he loved jumping in from the side, as he didn't do it when we first got there today. But after about ninety minutes of swimming, he climbed the stairs to get out, walked to the side, and did it.

"E!"

He jumped in several more times accompanied by the applause that H. and Anastasia and I awarded him for his courage. Just as we were about to wrap things up and go home, I saw him get out of the water once more, walk to the far edge of the patio, and run toward the water to finally vault in at a velocity he hadn't attempted before. As he was running, I almost sprang up from where I was sitting to keep him from doing so. I instead kept myself from intervening and found that faith, the faith that all parents have to find, sometimes right on the spot, that allows us to allow our children to grow despite our fear that they'll be harmed in the process.

"E!"

He made it.

Mornings

You sleep later than you used to
and hardly ever prowl in the middle
of the night
anymore.
I'm surprised at how
surprised I am by it. Sometimes
I think things will stay where they are today
forever.
But they don't. Ever.
I should know
better. I put your new bed
a double one, suitable for a grownup
by the window so
you can see the leaves

dance when you first open your eyes.

I Dream He Talks to Me

So you might see the sky
when you have your first thought.
When you don't wake by eight I
go into your bedroom to
check on you
If your eyes are closed and I know you
are sleeping I
let you continue
if I can
If they are fluttering and I know you
are awake I
lean down and tell you
good morning
You pull me in for a
hug a wide
smile spreads across your
sleepy beautiful face
you hold me
tight to your neck and face to
your heart
to you
If I ever doubt we
will get through
this with our dignity
intact with our backs as
straight as the sunflowers that you so
resemble
the mornings remind
me.

Water Pressure

He goes in and out the front and back doors of the house all day long and goes through typically no less than five wardrobe changes per day depending on how many times he gets in and out of his inflatable swimming pool in a twenty-four-hour period. That's fine. That's typical of most children who are lucky enough to have five sets of clothes and a home with a washer and dryer. It leaves me with a lot of laundry to do, but I let him go for it. However, a new clothing situation has developed.

A new clothing situation has developed and I don't know why. John Henry has lately gotten into the habit of repeatedly taking off his shorts and underwear and either standing at the window or the bathroom door in my bedroom, which now stays locked, or just roaming around with his bottom half unclothed. I don't know why except that it probably has something to do with his desire for water—he either wants to take a bath or go swimming and it's his way of letting me know. Mostly, he does it only in the house, but from time to time I'll look up and he's suddenly bare-assed in the front yard or on the front porch. Lately, this repetitive action occurs on average six or seven times a day.

This repetitive action occurs six or seven times a day and it requires of me my own repetitive action, as I have to find the shorts and underwear he has left somewhere and help him put them back on. He takes them off. I help him put them back on. He takes them off. I help him put them back on. Over and over. Over and over.

Over and over I imagine what must bring on this behavior—obsessive-compulsive disorder, anxiety so severe it makes him walk in circles, preoccupation with being in the water—he lives in a sort of loop of specific interests and repetitive actions in a world that has limited ability to engage with him. He does what's safe for him to do and what feels good for him to do. Any sort of interaction with water is at the top of the list of things that make him feel his safest best—it does not resist his movements but covers him with a weighty softness that calms his busy body when he can actually get in it, but even a stream from the faucet, a can of soda or bottle of water that he can pour out, or a puddle on the ground will do. He digs a behavioral trench and would prefer to stay in it all day long.

He digs a behavioral trench and would prefer to stay in it all day long and some days start earlier than others.

This morning he was awake at 5:15. I expected him to stay in bed until at least eight as is his habit of late, but he decided to get up with me today. I'd only gotten one sip of coffee down when I heard him in his room, raring to go. It was just as well. We ate breakfast, got dressed, drove the dog to the veterinarian and dropped him off for his checkup, then went back home. When we walked in the house, John Henry immediately went to my bathroom door, took off his shorts and underwear, and waited for me to let him in.

He took off his shorts and underwear and waited for me to let him in so that told me he wanted to take a bath. That was fine with me, so I unlocked the bathroom. We went in and I started the water for him. I helped him out of his shirt and made the sign for *headphones*. He took them off and gave them to me.

He took them off and gave them to me and that's the reason there's a lock on the door—to keep him out of the bathroom. He got in the tub. I pulled the bath mat far across the room to keep it from getting drenched. I placed a towel on the floor outside the tub to help absorb the splashes of water that I knew would probably soon be coming over its edge and racing toward the closet because we live in an old and unlevel house. I left the room and fetched my laptop, then returned to the bathroom to sit on the closed toilet seat so I could look over emails and tend to any that needed tending to. My plan is always to stay in the bathroom if I can, to try to keep him safe and from soaking the floor yet again.

He soaks the floor yet again.

"John Henry, please do not do that!"

Water splashed onto my laptop screen as he slammed his right arm down into the water like Bamm-Bamm from *The Flintstones* banging his club into the earth.

"Baby, please stop!"

He wouldn't stop. He then began a vigorous version of crickets—the knee pumping and rubbing together of his legs that he has done since he was an infant—that produced such a roil that it sent drops of water flying into my eyes.

It sent drops of water flying into my eyes and I thought about how many baths he's taken some days. I remember being snowed in when we lived in New York and not being able to go anywhere. I'd let him take four or five baths a day for something to do. Water entertains him. Maybe we can get a real swimming pool sometime soon but for now we go through seven or eight inflatables per summer. He likes to bite through the plastic, so they don't necessarily last long. When he's in the water he's happy. He'll stay in his pool for hours, then when he's ready to go inside he'll stand at the back door.

He'll stand at the back door and I'll walk him to my bathroom, where he prefers to bathe. He has his own bathroom but it has a smaller tub and a slower faucet. He takes off the shorts and underwear he's gotten wet in his swimming pool and I help him out of his shirt, then make the sign for *headphones*. He takes them off and gives them to me. He gets in the tub. I pull the bath mat far across the room to keep it from getting drenched. I place a towel on the floor outside the tub to help absorb the splashes of water that I know will probably soon be coming over its edge and racing toward the closet because we live in an old and unlevel house. My plan is always to stay in the bathroom if I can, to try to keep him safe and from soaking the floor yet again.

He soaks the floor yet again.

❧

He goes in and out the front and back doors of the house all day long and goes through typically no less than five wardrobe changes per day depending on how many times he gets in and out of his inflatable swimming pool in a twenty-four-hour period. That's fine. That's typical of most children who are lucky enough to have five sets of clothes and a home with a washer and dryer. It leaves me with a lot of laundry to do, but I let him go for it. However, a new clothing situation has developed.

St. Jude Lives in the Garden Now

I sit in a chair on the front porch with you and watch your face. You sit in the swing across from me. It moves toward me, then slightly back, while you hold the string that is attached to the Scooby-Doo balloon we bought at Kroger two days ago. You look out into the yard where the dogs piddle around. I wonder what you're thinking.

How do I explain death to you?

"You have another angel now."

That's the only way I can say it. My mouth refuses to make any other words. You smiled a smile I've seen before when I said it on Tuesday, before we went to get Popsicles and the balloon. It was the smile that makes your face look like there's nothing you don't already know. Maybe you did already know that he was going, and that he had gone, sooner than the rest of us did. I remember asking myself if you were worried about him when you got so upset right after bedtime that night three or four weeks ago.

Is he worried about his brother?

I was, but I always was, since the day I met him almost twenty years ago. Your father was, he always was too, and for much longer than anyone else—he was his firstborn, twenty-eight years older than you. Your half brother, but we never call him that. Now that he has shifted his energy, so do we. Where to, I don't know yet.

There has already been too much loss in your life. The holes in me should not be part of your inheritance, but I know you feel them. I know you feel them in me. And now there is another in us. This time, a deeper one for you, I'm afraid. Blood is blood. I'm so sorry and sorry isn't a good enough word to say how sorry I am. But we mustn't dwell, my sweet boy, and you live that better and truer than any other person I know. One of the best things you've taught me is how to be right where I am right when I'm there.

I look, a few times a day now, at the photographs of him holding you. There's the one on the street in New York City when you were three. I hung a copy of it in your bedroom. There's the one at the festival in California when you were six. When you were smaller he'd always scoop you up and twirl you around. You would both laugh and smile and look right at each other, right through each other. I hate that you can't hear his laugh anymore. I trust you've kept it in your memories.

Yesterday I took your hands, still smaller than mine though your feet are not, and put them in the dirt in the garden bed we picked as the perfect spot for the statue of St. Jude. The Saint of Lost Causes.

It can watch you play.

It can watch you splash in the new swimming pool.

It can watch you grow, even if your brother cannot anymore.

Not from here anyway.

Who will tell you when I die? When you hear the news, will you smile the same smile? Maybe you already know that balloons are easier to hold on to than people.

Dream #4

The sun was about to rise. I wished so badly to go back to sleep to hear you again, though I was not able. I lay there with my eyes closed, the nimbus remaining in the air, still trying to go back, go back, go back to hear more, more, more. I thought about your voice.

> *I like blueberry waffles, bacon, and a bit of fruit for breakfast. I can't always eat the hard-boiled eggs you make me first thing in the morning because they sometimes turn my stomach.*

That's what I remembered most. You told me a lot of things that went out of my mind with the fluttering of my eyelashes, as if they batted each memory away. I wanted to hold on to them. I tried. I wanted to remember every utterance. I couldn't.

It was not an easy dream. It wasn't as wonderful, hearing you speak, as it has most times been. Your spirit was not as light as it has always otherwise appeared to be in my sleep. Not dark, no, not at all, rather just deeper. *Deep* is the only word I can conjure to describe the feeling. Your countenance bore concern, and more than a hint of gravitas better suited to a worried, middle-aged man than a ten-year-old boy.

It settled down on me like a question-mark-shaped heaviness that has been strapped to my shoulders since 6 a.m. I can't remember anything else you said but the thing about breakfast even though I know you told me some other things I'd like to know. I can't remember the words but I remember the feeling. I have a sense of the collective weight. Maybe your birthday brought some knowledge of your maturity, your approaching adolescence and manhood. Maybe I cannot remember what you said because my mind is protecting me from some knowing you imparted. It will come back to me. When I'm ready, it will.

Terms of Surrender

A great singer is he who sings our silences.
                                    —Kahlil Gibran

Spring 2020. The beginning of the COVID-19 pandemic. We were hunkered down in quarantine like the rest of the world, trying to figure out how to navigate such an abrupt change. All of our gigs had been canceled. John Henry's school had closed and he was back in Tennessee. I was worried, but happy we were safe, home, and together until further notice. We were okay.

I'd already hired John Henry's summer team. We had a great ABA teacher as well as his longtime speech therapist on board, but neither was starting with us until mid-May, when we'd planned to begin before everything shut down. It was just as well. We took the idea of social distance to heart and were as safe as we could be in those early days, but we had to keep John Henry on track in the interim. His New York teachers quickly figured out how to do Zoom sessions with all the students, so we began to do schoolwork at home—two ABA sessions, one speech therapy session, and one occupational therapy session per day, all thirty minutes each. His father took Mondays and Tuesdays at his house, and I took Wednesday through Friday at ours. Ten minutes before each session, I'd locate the needed materials from the list that was emailed the night before, lead John Henry to the work area in his bedroom, and log in.

Nonidentical matching would go like this: I'd place four items—let's say a fork, a cup, a shirt, and a shoe—in a line on the table. Then I would hand John Henry a different kind of fork than the one on the table and say, "Match." He would match the fork in his hand to the other one, and so on for the other items on the table, or "in the field," as it's called. Identical matching worked the same way except the items were exact replicas.

When I'd watch his eyes scan the table carefully, he'd almost always match the items perfectly. When I watched his eyes wander, he wouldn't. Attending is his main issue. He's a hard worker, but shows no real interest, as if he sees no meaning or need in learning the letters of the alphabet or why it's important to know that two different types of forks are still both forks. The possibilities that he might know it all already, that his brain just doesn't work that way, or that these sorts of things are meaningless to him have occurred to me as he has certainly shown signs of each, but until we know more about that, we keep going.

He needs the structure, the routine that he's so used to regardless of his displayed level of concern.

We'd work our way through three or four trials, then he'd earn his reinforcer—his reward—and get to spend some time with it before we'd start the next. Some days it was a battle to get the sessions done and I began to dread them. I know he did too. The redirecting was constant. He'd get up from the worktable and flop on his bed, try to hide inside his closet or his hanging swing, or even ask to go to the bathroom to get out of work, no matter what I tempted him with. I've always appreciated his teachers and therapists and was reminded of their hard work every time we sat down for a session, but I envied their lack of emotional involvement in John Henry's performance. I know they care about how he does, but of course my attachment to the outcome of it all is far deeper. When the last session was over each day I'd breathe a sigh of relief. I tried to find satisfaction that we'd done the best we could and let go of thoughts about the outcome of everything. I've always known I needed to do that but such balance hasn't very often been available to me.

&

I play music in the house almost always. That spring was no different. I'd been on a Hiss Golden Messenger kick for probably a week or so when I noticed I'd latched on to *Terms of Surrender*, the newest album, and would put it on almost every night while I made dinner. When I find music I like, I tend to listen to it almost constantly until I know it by heart. I'll then move on from it, but once it's in my bloodstream I use it like a reference book and access it when I need to identify an emotion I can't quite name without the help of a tune. I listened to the title track on repeat a lot. It's a beautiful song—the simple, melancholy piano, the economy of phrase, and the longing in the vocal are stunning—but it had me in its grip in an unusual way, in a way that only happens every two or three years. I needed to hear it, to internalize it, to add it to that pile of references I use so often. It felt like a reflection of some sort. It made me think about the rhythm of our days, about how we got where we are, about where we're going. I wondered if quarantine was offering a glimpse of our future—is this what life will be like after John Henry isn't in school anymore? Will we always struggle to get through ABA sessions and continue to have difficulty communicating? Though I've certainly thought about and tried to prepare myself for the idea that we might live together for the rest of my life, it's been an abstract idea waiting in the distance. Something about that period, when one day smeared into the next and the next, made me see more clearly and closely how it might actually be. *These are my terms, terms of surrender . . .* It rang in my head. Music sometimes says what I can't put my finger on.

I was grateful that we were okay. I wanted to push through and not admit how tired I really was. I'd wake up every morning feeling great despite everything, but would be so worn out at the end of each day that I'd fall asleep mid-sentence when H. and I would try to catch up with each other. I worried about how the school sessions were going. I worried about realizing how important it is to me that John Henry show constant progress. I began to question my own point of view in a way that I never had before. Why was I so wrapped up in results and conclusions? And how could I be sure the supposed path toward those results and conclusions was the right one? I see him beam when he does well and is praised and rewarded. I also see him cry with frustration and anger when he isn't interested or if he feels something is too challenging or if he just isn't in the mood. I know we have to push our children, but sometimes it all feels like too much.

Where is the line between enough and too much? Between what he needs and what we want, between helping and hurting, between just enough and diminishing returns, between pushing for the realization of potential and trying to change who someone is because his edges don't fit into the world's man-made round hole? We helpers are so wrapped up in what *we* think, so convinced that we're doing the right thing by leading those who are different from us down the path *we* choose—which is always the one that leads to supposedly more normal—that we sometimes don't stop to think about what those we're helping might have to say.

Is it fair for him to be constantly pushed? Is it fair for any parent to push any child? I don't know, and I know most parents do the best they can. But the truth is, there is no absolute certainty that any of the things we do make a huge difference. It's hard to see the micro-shifts and easy to wonder about the viability of going back to Goliath with a slingshot day after day. However, our routine and regimen is the only attack we know of that will lead to the best life for John Henry and I'm okay with that for the most part. I also shudder to think about what life would be like had we not taken the route that we have. I know, at the end of the day, that it's not the huge difference at once that counts, but the fact that all of those little rocks we shoot might knock the giant out from time to time. We stay in the groove as much as there can be one and hope we're someday as triumphant as David. Better a few rocks at a time than no rocks at all. But there are some days when I want to wave the white flag and throw down these flimsy weapons, these tiny pebbles that seem so underpowered—the routines, the schedules, the embedded techniques, the constant facilitation of communication, the countdowns, the timer, the list of receptive ID objects, the reinforcers, the reading, the researching, the management of every little thing to try to control life so we don't lose what progressions we *have* made, the planning for the worst and hoping for the best. Maybe you just have to give sometimes. Cry uncle. Learn how to live under occupation. *Surrender.*

❦

Autism is a disorder, not a disease. It wrote itself into my son. Who am I—*who are we*—to try to change that for him? How do I know that he wants to be changed? I have to ask that question while I'm making all of these decisions for him. I know that's part of the dance that every parent dances no matter their child's characteristics. But more than I know that, I know my son's life is his. I have to remember that even in the chilling opacity of the darkest moments. I can't say that I always have. I have not surrendered. I've fought autism with everything I have. If that means I've fought him, fought who he is, that makes me ashamed. Is that truly living, or white-knuckling? Is that accepting what we've got and making the best of it, or living under a shroud of *what if today is the day all of this changes*?

The changes we envisioned at the beginning haven't come. The stims go away but are replaced with others. The words he once had haven't reappeared in a meaningful way. The voice isn't ever going to return. A new one may emerge, but that little vocabulary, his original voice, those sweet baby utterances that have haunted me so much and that we've tried so hard to recover, are gone. I'll never forget them.

Ball

Beau

Petey

Cracker

Go

Bath

Duck

Daddy

Mama

Hey
Baby
Apple
Happy
Feet
Head
Bubble
Cat
Cow
Circle
Turkey
Banana
Dang
Yay
Juice
Eye
Ear
Up
Bird

Or their absence.
His voice was there. Then it was gone.
I have to let it go. I have to let it be gone.

I envision writing down the words on scraps of paper,
burning each one, and burying the ashes in the ground.
Goodbye.

⌒

Terms of surrender. It stuck in my brain. What are my terms with this, now that we are here?

Peace. I want to make peace with it and I realize I never have. But what does that even mean? Does it mean stopping all of this constant therapy? Does it mean ending the search for the right methods to help him emerge? Does it mean giving up hope that he will gain independence? What would life be like if I let that hope slip away from us? What would *we* be like?

Life would be, and we would be, unrecognizable. I can't imagine how tired I would be if I didn't have hope that my son will find his way to his most realized self, if I didn't have hope, period. But even hope sometimes gets heavy; I guess that's why it seems to belong to the strongest of us. It can't exist on its own. It has to be bolstered by action lest it wither. There are days I don't know which action to take anymore. How do I simultaneously try to change him and let him be who he is? I know I have to trust the process and path we've taken. I also know I have to find a way to keep traveling on it and let go of what we think we're moving toward at the same time. There is a difference between having a relationship with what someone does and having a relationship with who someone is.

⌒

Letting go of outcomes is not my strong suit. I've spent my life trying to control results to make sure I don't get hurt. Trauma, and I've had my share of it, does that to a person—we get our ass knocked in the dirt and then learn to focus on doing everything we can to keep from going down again. But we *do* go down, over and over, flailing incredulously at the pain that we tell ourselves we can keep from coming to us if we just do everything like we're supposed to . . . if we just hold our mouths right and stand on one foot while we hold our fists up to life . . . if we just . . . if we just . . . if we just . . .

The only way I've found to get through it with any grace at all is to be open to it all—the love, the fear, the agony, the joy, the horrifying thoughts that our children might not be okay without us—and understand that life is wild and uncontrollable. As many times as that has hit me in the face, I've been stubborn and have tried to bargain with it, telling myself if I just . . . if I just . . . if I just . . . There is no bargain to strike. I have nothing to offer the whirlwind of life and it doesn't appreciate my unwillingness to get caught up in its tumult. It has shown me time and time again to ride the waves wholeheartedly or get broken due to resistance.

The teacher shows up when we're ready to learn the lesson.

⌒

Autism is just as much a part of my son as his blue eyes and long fingers. What I want to surrender is always trying to change that because what I see now, now that we are here, is that it isn't the work but instead the relentless effort to eradicate autism that's exhausting. What I want to surrender is the constant pursuit of the idea that he might become less who he is and more someone else. Autism is here with us, here in him, and it isn't going anywhere.

I might've said, even as recently as a few months ago, that if I had it my way John Henry would be as typical as they come. I might even still say that some days now because the vision I have of him playing in hidden creeks and streams, catching frogs and snakes and throwing dirt clods at his friends, overstaying his welcome at their houses and testing their parents' patience, spending too much time playing video games, and starting a rock band in the garage sounds easier than the life we have now. That vision isn't what we've got. We aren't having an ordinary experience. But what we are having is something more extraordinary than I dreamed—we get to see life from an unusual, remarkable angle. I get to know a kind of love and healing that I never could've known any other way. For me, that is a privilege and I won't get the peace I so desire until I see and treat it as such. If you asked me today if I'd change my son, the answer would be no, not unless that's what he wanted. I want him exactly as he is, however that is.

Acceptance is the deal we make when we want to stop fighting. Acceptance for me is allowing my son to be the version of himself that he is right now, because there *is* only right now. Choosing to see it that way is the only part of this over which I really have any power at all. I don't want my son's disability to tear us up. I have to love every bit of him in order to love him as he deserves.

Acceptance is being here, right now, instead of looking ahead to the day when this will all be over. It isn't going to be over.

Acceptance is being here instead of looking ahead to the day when I "get my son back." I already have my son, and in full.

Acceptance is being here instead of looking ahead to the day when the thick terror of uncertainty is thinned to a more sustainable degree. Only I can control how scared I'm willing to be.

Today is the day. Today can always be the day that all of this changes if I change the way I see it.

There is no worse helplessness than the kind a parent feels when they can't fix things for their child. If I could give John Henry my voice, my regulation, my ability to pass through the world with a certain amount of ease, I would. I can't. He might not even want them. My baby has autism. He probably always will. That doesn't mean giving up hope that he will thrive in a million different ways, but it does mean that I have to let hope breathe and float instead of suffocating and weighing it down with my expectations and an unrealistic vision of a life of ease and no hurt. Hope won't matter at all if I make it into a burden, if I see it as something that can only hold an idea of my son as a different person than who he is. Hope lives in the very motes in his marrow. It isn't up to me to try to alter his life according to my will; it is only up to me to respect him and help him on his path, and I can only pray that

I use my best judgment and the most empathy, respect, compassion, and love to guide him in the right directions. To that honor and to this life I wholeheartedly surrender lest I risk living it kicking and screaming at the utter viciousness we sometimes encounter simply by being here.

These are my terms, terms of surrender . . .

⁓

Art is a mirror. It has been my healing over and over again. I suspect it is and will be for John Henry as well. When I see him as he is, I am strengthened by the profoundly beautiful, strong, and intrepid person who chose me to be his mama. He is happy, he is full of magic, and he is the truest piece of art I've ever had the privilege to witness. When I see him, I see that he is already whole. When I see us, I see that I am too. I see that *we* are. We are wholly us and that us is for me to embrace. Maybe one day this will all be less of a mystery to me. Or maybe the cracks and crevices will become deeper and I'll just continue to get better at letting them be. Either way, we're gonna be okay. Either way, I pray I'll always keep listening, and not only to my dreams.

Acknowledgments

Thank you, Laura Lynn Smith Moorer, for being the kind of mama that you were. Though you are gone, your strength and tenderness live in me. Your smile and sweet spirit lives in John Henry. Thank you for watching over us.

Thank you, Laura Dolbear Smith, Marie Dolbear McQuorquodale, and Jane Smith Courtois, for filling in every gap you could in Mama's absence.

Thank you, Shelby Lynn Moorer, for knowing without me saying and for unconditional, fierce love.

Thank you, Dr. Alice H. Frederick, for invaluable guidance and lessons in character and perseverance.

Thank you, Ashley Larrimore Bronzi (Leelee), for showing me and loving me.

Thank you, Traci Thomas, for your strength and heart.

Thank you, Jessica Haedge, Kaylee Evers, Austin Sawyer, Jessica Doran, Kayla Jackson, Nicole Harper, Carolyn Chui, Jacqueline Aguilar, Amy Mason, Miranda Farabaugh, Ashley Mandell, Jacqueline Hickey, Ivy Feldman, John Lam, Aaron Wing, Christine Prush, Aksana Plotnikava, Beau Lopez, Emily Lerner, Beth Cannistraci, Laura Prestia, Juli Liske, Dr. Zach Warren, and every other therapist, educator, administrator, and medical professional who has helped and continues to help us figure out the best routes to the best life.

Thank you to everyone in our wonderful and kind extended musical family and beyond who has kept an eye out and a hand held while Mama or Daddy had to pick up an instrument and sing a few.

Thank you, MC Taylor, for the inspiration for "Terms of Surrender."

Thank you, Emily Earle.

Thank you to my Mama tribe.

Thank you, Renée Sedliar, for your sensitive eye and tender heart.

Thank you, Laura Nolan, for your belief in me and for your love of our family.

Thank you, Hayes Carll, for your understanding, patience, encouragement, love, and for being the best Pop-Pop there is.

Thank you, Steve Earle.

Thank you, John Henry Earle, for being the reason. You are my shining star forevermore.

Dream #3

Your voice sounds like it does when we're awake — lilting, soft, sweet, yet boyish and quietly authoritative. You ask questions but are certain at the same time, not of the answers, but of the solidity of mystery. You're knowing that our waking world's definition of truth and too slippery for anyone to hold onto is as bright as a springtime day and as heavy as midnight. You appear to want to confuse, but I sense you are artfully reminding me through our questions.

I thought for a second that it could've been real. I thought about how we'd talked. I thought about your voice and I lay there, trying to burn the sound into my brain so that I wouldn't forget it. How could I forget it? I never do. But I still went over it again and again as my tears fell and I let go, little by little of the hope that you might say something when you opened your eyes.

Maybe it won't be today. But I know the day will come in whatever way that it does. To that, I hold on.